Words of Praise for Stay CALM
(The book and the Method)

I've seen firsthand the results of people using the Stay CALM Method™. When Jon Forrest taught the method to our customer care agents, our customer satisfaction scores went to their highest levels ever.

—**Victor Tsao, Entrepreneur, co-founder of Linksys now Cisco-Linksys**

This book is a treasure! It blends the best of the philosophy of Aikido and the time-tested lessons of good communication in a very tidy package.

—**Sensei James Nakayama, Western Regional Director, Aikido Association of America**

I am amazed at how many useful tools for better communicating are packed into this small but powerful work. Stay CALM Method™ has helped several of my juries to break deadlocks and settle important cases. I read this book over and over.

—**An attorney in Alaska**

Our plant continues to benefit from the work of Jon Forrest and his Stay CALM Method™, we have been experiencing higher ratings on our employee satisfaction scores and people are communicating with much better results.

—**Tom Willis, Director of Training, Neutrogena, a Division of J&J**

The principles contained in this book are timeless and I can easily apply the Stay CALM Method™, even when the proverbial fan gets hit with the stuff... And the flash cards really drove home the main points. This is something that anyone can easily use to improve their relationships.
—**Bob White, VP, Global Enterprise Initiatives of a Fortune 50 Company**

This book and the Stay CALM Method™ made an instant, positive impact on our leadership team and now our entire organization has embraced this work, it's that good, and very simple too.
—**Ron Holecek, CEO, WATG Architecture & Design**

About the Book

You Can Win and No One Has to Lose

People who have developed the ability to communicate effectively, even under stress or in conflict, get promoted faster, keep their marriages intact, have more friends and enjoy better health. If you want an easy to remember and effective method for dealing with tough talks and awful arguments, keep reading.

Whether it's your boss, a co-worker, your spouse, a family member or a friend, people in our lives sometimes come at us with words that cause us harm. With this book you will discover how to effectively transform these verbal assaults using powerful and simple tools to manage the confrontation.

This book introduces a reliable approach for "blending" with anger, frustration and hostility so you actually transform your adversary into your ally and together discover a workable solution. What's more, it shows how to integrate easy-to-learn techniques so they become your natural response.

Described here is Jon Forrest's innovative *Stay CALM Method*™. It is a way to fully protect yourself, your image and self-esteem—while at the same time winning the respect of everyone else involved, including the person who attacked you.

Drawing from a wide range of disciplines and new findings in the physiology of communication, the method combines the principles of Aikido, a non-combative martial art with the teachings of such greats as Dale Carnegie, Stephen Covey, Daniel Goleman, Marshall Rosenberg and Dr. Suzette Haden Elgin. The result is a brilliant fusion of principles and practices that allow you to protect yourself without harming others psychically, socially or emotionally.

Stay CALM: Verbal Aikido Turns Arguments Into Agreements, reveals how to:
- **Recognize and respond to verbal attacks, both subtle and obvious**
- **Determine what the upset person is really after (it's one of only 4 things!)**
- **Evaluate personality types to know what behavior to use to get results**
- **Come out of a potentially damaging situation feeling great about yourself**

The *Stay CALM Method*™ is fully explained in these pages. The book provides all you need to know so you can effectively use this streamlined approach to conflict resolution for the 21st century. It guides you through an innovative approach to handling communication breakdowns that is highly effective and produces positive results and beneficial, win-win outcomes.

When conversation turns to confrontation, you could get angry and reactive and try to overpower your adversary . . . or you could take the verbal beating, feeling your frustration and blood pressure rise and your self-esteem and pride deflate. Finally there's a new alternative: read *Stay CALM* and walk away a healthy, happy hero.

Life is too short and relationships are too valuable to do anything less than *Stay CALM*.

About the Author

Jon Forrest began reading books on human behavior at age 10 and has continued his exploration of human potential and interpersonal relationships throughout his life. At the age of 13 he began his study and practice of Aikido, a Japanese martial art that teaches redirecting force to create harmony with, rather than to defeat or dominate attackers. He has successfully integrated these two disciplines into a practical approach for highly effective communication and personal interaction especially under stress and in conflict situations. Jon is CEO of iCAN International, a firm that provides coaching, consulting and training in effective communication, business strategy, and leadership to improve bottom line results, for companies and individuals worldwide. Jon lives in Southern California with his wife and family.

When conversation turns to confrontation...

Stay CALM

Verbal Aikido Turns Arguments Into Agreements

Jon Forrest

When conversation turns to confrontation
Stay CALM
Verbal Aikido turns arguments into agreements

Published by iCAN Media
16485 Laguna Canyon Road, Suite 110
Irvine, CA 92618

orders@icanmedia.tv
www.icanmedia.tv

Text Copyright © 2004, 2006, 2007 by Jon Forrest.
Photographs © 2004 by Jon Forrest.
All rights reserved. Published by iCAN Media.

No part of this publication may be reproduced in whole or in part, or stored in a retrieval system, or transmitted in any form or by any means, electronic, mechanical, photocopying, recording, or otherwise, without permission in writing from the publisher, except by a reviewer who may quote brief passages in a review.

ISBN-13: 978-0-9759357-2-9
ISBN-10: 0-9759357-2-0
Library of Congress Control Number: 2005933293

10 9 8 7 6 5 4 3 2 1
Printed in the U.S.A.
Third edition, revised 2007

Cover and interior design by Lightbourne, Inc.
Videography for Flip Art™ by TLB Productions
iCAN Media and Flip Art™ logos by Travis Hanson

Library of Congress Cataloging-in-Publication Data

Forrest, Jon.

    Stay calm : verbal aikido turns arguments into agreements / Jon Forrest. -- Upd. ed. -- Mission Viejo, CA : iCAN Media, 2007.

    p. ; cm.

    ISBN: 978-0-9759357-2-9
    The book includes "flip art" graphics on the back of each page. When "thumbed", the images resemble a movie showing Aikido motion.
    Includes bibliographical references.

    1. Conflict management. 2. Interpersonal conflict. 3. Interpersonal relations. 4. Communication--Psychological aspects. 5. Aikido. I. Title. II. Title: Verbal aikido.

HM1126 .F67 2007
303.6/9--dc22   0711

What do these words mean to you?

Manipulate
Intimidate
Outburst
Retaliate
Vengeance
Persuade
Resistance
Withhold
Control
Interrupt
Avoid
Embarrass
Attack

If you have an emotional reaction to any of these words, they are probably words that relate to negative or upsetting interpersonal experiences that you have had in the past.

Stay CALM was written to help you gain new skills to understand and relate to other people, and reduce or even eliminate these types of experiences in your life.

C.A.L.M.

Communicative
Being communicative includes the entire spectrum of interaction through kinesthetic, auditory, and visual channels. All meaning in life occurs as a result of communication. The ability to be communicative enables us to create meaning through shared experience with other people.

Aikido
Aikido is a non-combative martial art founded in Japan in the 1940's by Morihei Ueshiba. The three kanji that make up the word Ai Ki Do essentially translate to: "The Way of the Harmonious Spirit." The core philosophy in Aikido is transforming Budo, the art of war, into the art of love. Accepting an attack by blending with the attacker's energy allows the Aikidoist to protect him or herself *and* the attacker from harm.

Leadership
Socrates declared that, above all, "Know Thyself." From that we might discover the directive to "Lead Yourself," to set an example, to model the great principles and philosophies of all time. Any serious attempt to better understand ourselves and our relation to others yields a leader.

Method
Defined as the pursuit of a process or a way by which we operate to effect and respond to change in ourselves and in the world around us.

Contents

About the Book	iii
About the Author	vi
C.A.L.M.	x
Dedication	xiii
Foreword	xv
Introduction	xvii
Foundation	1
Cornerstones	7
A Platform of Compassion	23
Human Behavior	47
The Method	65
Blend (Part One)	81
Real Feelings	103
Blend (Part Two)	111
Neutralize & Guide	147
Debugging	165
Onward	177
Suggested Reading	181
About iCAN International	184
The Products of iCAN Media	186

Dedication

First and foremost, this book is dedicated to my father, who, if he were still alive, would have delighted in writing a foreword for this, my first book. His influence on my life is immeasurable. I have always said that if I could be even half the man my father was I'd have reason to be proud. His ability to show the way without resorting to lecture or punishment set a standard for living life that awed and inspired those who knew him. As a child psychologist and family counselor, the impact he had on the people he touched was immense and evidenced by the pilgrimage that visited him at his deathbed. They came to pay homage. There were folks from all walks of life whose lives and whose children's lives had been ushered to a much higher level of harmony by the words, and even more, by the example of my father, Don Bowlus.

And to my mother, Faith, whose unconditional love still provides incredible support and energy for my work, and whose writing style heavily influenced my own. Your spirituality is reflected in this book.

And to my wonderful wife Cindie, who provides the perfect combination of support and confidence to keep me focused. Her belief in our ability to contribute meaningfully to the people in our lives, and her grounded and honest reflection, provides unbounded inspiration and encouragement. You are a great teacher.

And to Michael Denisoff, who has helped me with this project; Nakayama Sensei for showing me the way of Aikido; Eddy Chister, who came up with the CALM acronym; my network of local editors who helped me refine this book; the professional help from Graham Van Dixhorne, Ellen Shepherd, Sheryll Alexander and Bob Swingle who all helped to make the book legitimate; colleagues, friends, and all the people with whom I have shared this method. Your ideas and discoveries are all in these pages. This book is dedicated to each of you. Thank you.

Foreword

I studied Aikido back in the mid-1970s. Back then few knew about it. I knew it was a soft martial art. It wasn't hard like karate or judo, which I also studied. In Aikido you used an opponent's energy to defend yourself, often tossing the assailant aside with a dance like move and a brush of your hand.

But no one ever told me back then that Aikido had interpersonal lessons and self-defense advice for off the mat, too. That's where Jon Forrest rides in with this wise book, Stay Calm.

I suppose the title says it all, though there are numerous levels of understanding when it comes to using "verbal Aikido" in arguments. That's why you need this book. It offers tips and insights into human behavior and the psychology of persuasion that aren't seen very often anywhere else.

His four cornerstones of human interaction are worth the price of admission. They can help you in any conversation, confrontation, or outright argument. They can help you easily navigate the encounters you already have with people in all situations, from the line at the store or the service person who refuses to give you a refund to the angry boss or flippant employee.

Jon has been in personal growth for more than three decades. He's learned a lot. Now he wants to bring harmony to the home and workplace. I believe he'll do it, too. After all, who am I to argue with the verbal aikido master?

I love this book. It's a quick read, with memorable pictures and stories to bring the points to life.

Read it and win—on and off the mat of life.

—**Dr. Joe Vitale, Author,** *The Attractor Factor*
A star of "The Secret" and "The Opus"
www.mrfire.com

Introduction

The trouble with most conflict resolution techniques is just that: they're techniques. They sound great when you read them or see them in a training class or video, but just when you need them the most—when conflict occurs—you can't recall them. The pressure of being in a volatile conversation makes it nearly impossible for our brains to access techniques and remember new phrases or specific scripts.

Though it may not happen often, these highly charged encounters with people who have lost self-control, where we feel attacked and victimized, are some of the most negative experiences in our lives. The resulting anguish and torment that follows such an attack can stay with us for days, weeks, even years, damaging our self-esteem and impairing our self-confidence.

In our professional lives, attacks like this by managers or executives can result in low morale and poor performance due to stifled creativity and an environment of fear and oppression. In our personal lives, attacks from family members or friends can force us to shut down to the experience of real love and nurturing relationships.

When we are verbally attacked, we are devalued and made to feel unworthy. Our sense of importance is undermined, and we feel misunderstood and hurt by the attacker's insensitivity to our feelings and needs.

Communicative Aikido Leadership Method, or CALM, which is based in large part on the martial art of Aikido, offers a method for staying in control when facing a verbal attack. Rather than "resisting" would-be opponents, Aikidoists can connect to the incoming energy and "blend" with attackers. This shifts the perspective from a confrontation to a partnership. By using the *Stay CALM Method*™ when you are attacked, you will be able to:

- **Prevent the conflict from escalating**
- **Remain in a leadership role**
- **Support and guide the attacker to regain self-control.**

In this book, you will learn about the four cornerstones upon which you can build a strong foundation for using the *Stay CALM Method*™. This will be your new place from which to deal with verbal attacks both subtle and obvious. You will explore principles from Aikido, including "Tenkan," which teaches a method for blending with and neutralizing an attacker's energy, and understanding different behavior styles. This will help you to understand how different people relate and give clarity to

Introduction

the concept of "personality clashes." Finally, you will look at different types of verbal attacks and conflict scenarios, both covert and overt. This book will aid you to discover the connection between your own state of being, your feelings and needs, and those of the people with whom you struggle to communicate.

This book is about dealing with people who have *temporarily* lost their self-control and are unable to stay calm while seeking a resolution to problems or issues.

It is not about dealing with people who are predisposed to unreasonable violent behaviors or people who are in need of professional intervention.

Studies have shown conclusive evidence that the benefits of being empathetic and compassionate toward our fellow man are enormous. Our health is better, our lifespan increases, our ability to maintain a close circle of supportive friends and family all improve as a result of our increased capacity for compassion.

When we are able to show someone by example what acceptance looks like, we are far more likely to find the similarities that unite us and we are less likely to focus on the differences that drive us apart.

Certainly we all know people who strain to maintain control over everything and everyone in their lives. They find fault in nearly everyone. For these people, friends and family members are usually few and far between, having withered and vanished under the glare of disdain regularly brandished by this type of individual.

Stay CALM

Look to the end of the line and think hard. Will you look back with a glad heart at the memories you've created and know that you have brought the people in your life happiness and shared with them the joys of this brief experience? What will folks say about you after you pass on?

Decide what you want to be known for, what kind of a person you want the world to see, and you will likely discover that the principles contained in this book may provide keys to creating a life that is truly fulfilling and reflects the person you want to be.

The "Flip-Art" on the back of these pages can be viewed by thumbing the pages quickly and smoothly with your left hand, from back to front, to see "movies" of an Aikido response to an attack.

Foundation

Foundation

The reason why principles work when techniques fail is that principles are the ultimate source or cause of any action. The concepts you learn from this book will work when you adopt them as core philosophies and key personal values.

As in a political campaign, if you are truly seeking to win the election and become a CALM Leader, you will need to adopt a "platform." The following chapter explains the Four Cornerstones of Human Interaction upon which you can establish a Platform of Compassion. Ultimately, it is our compassion towards people that will determine our effectiveness in relating to them.

Compassion is defined as the ability to show, by your graceful tolerance, a gentle mercy toward as broad a range of humanity as you can possibly muster, no matter your personal preferences.

There's a saying (and trust me, I'm full of 'em) that 95% of people believe they are in the top 5% of people who have great people skills. This is because we judge how well we get along with other people based on the people with whom we get along well.

Once you have gained a basic understanding of the *Stay CALM Method*™, you will be able to find opportunities to develop your new skills by identifying the people in your life towards whom you find it difficult to extend compassion. That's a good place to begin.

I will share an example of this type of relationship so you have a point of reference for applying these four cornerstones.

Foundation

I managed a transmission repair shop once while recovering from a long entrepreneurial adventure (I'm a serial entrepreneur). One of the technicians, Benny, and I got along really well. I did not have total compassion for him though; his lifestyle choices were such that I found it difficult to fully accept this young man, even though my "managerial" skills enabled me to have rapport to ensure a smooth working relationship.

That lack of true acceptance and real compassion showed itself in a particularly sticky situation with a minor repair. It turned out to be a major repair, and then was not able to be completed by Christmas as promised. To further compound the situation, the customer really needed to use the car to travel to see his ailing mother for the holiday.

Benny snapped at me for pushing him over this repair and I laid into him in retaliation without thinking about what the situation was like for him. That one slip was enough to unveil my cleverly hidden lack of real acceptance and understanding of Benny, not just in this situation, but overall as a person. It took months to get back to a decent working relationship and the friendship never really recovered. I learned a lot from that breakdown.

I failed to make a choice in how I viewed Benny—based on the Four Cornerstones of Human Interaction—that would have provided valuable tools to help me respond to this situation with more compassion and awareness. As the attacker in this scenario, I can only wish for a do-over. As the recipient of the attack, I can only imagine the distrust and pain Benny felt (and may still feel).

Cornerstones

Cornerstones

These Cornerstones are simple but not simplistic. By that I mean that they may seem intuitive and commonsense but you most likely have never seen them compiled and linked together in this fashion. It is my hope that this chapter will help you take these concepts from a sub-language level to a conscious language level of understanding. In putting language to these fundamental principles and applying them daily, you will have won half the battle in staying calm in the face of verbal attacks.

Cornerstone #1
What Everybody Wants

There are two universal needs that human beings everywhere need to satisfy in order to be fulfilled in their relationships with others. They transcend age, race, religion, nationality, and culture:

1) Everybody wants to feel important.
2) Everybody wants to be understood.

Those are the two big drivers for the human race. The saying (see? I told you I was full of 'em) that sums this up is:
> *People don't care how much you know,*
> *'Til they know how much you care.*

I've mentioned this already, and will bring it up several more times to make sure you have it clearly in mind: CALM is principle-based—not technique-based—so you will need to make a shift in the way you "believe," in the

face of conflict, not just in the way you "act." Seek to make other people feel important and prove to them that you want to understand them, and you will notice that there are fewer and fewer conflicts occurring in your relationships.

Cornerstone #2
The Internal Dialogue

When you are first learning to walk as a baby, every time you fall, everyone cheers and claps and encourages you to get up and try it again. This support in our failures and encouragement to keep trying is intuitive for adult humans supporting baby humans.

Then our schooling begins, and all that changes. Now you get praise and recognition only when you do things right! When you make a mistake, you get marked down. When you make a big enough mistake, you get chastised and made to feel bad about yourself and your performance.

This is all taking place just at the time when you are beginning to develop language skills. So now, when you are just finding out about "mistakes," you create a story inside your head about what kind of person you are when you fail. This story, and the decisions you made about yourself, are likely to still be with you today and they may show up in the way you talk to yourself when you blunder. It was Will Rogers who said, "If someone talked to you the way you talk to yourself, you'd punch 'em in the nose!"

So here's step one towards resolving conflict: Begin talking to yourself like you would a dear loved one. If *you*

don't, who will? There is no law that says you have to beat yourself up when you blow it. In fact, you will probably recover more quickly from your mistakes if you take Anthony Robbins' advice. He tells us that the quality of one's life can largely be determined by the quality of one's mistakes. If you want a better life, make better mistakes. Or put another way, *the path to wisdom is experience . . . the path to experience is mistakes.*

So PLEASE, will you accept my invitation to talk nicely to yourself? I promise you will enjoy far greater peace and joy when you are more compassionate in the way you speak to yourself.

When the fight inside resolves, the fight outside dissolves.

Cornerstone #3
The Cosmic Joke

O.K., here's the deal. All of us are scared silly of what other people think about us. I see it every time I'm working with a group for the first time and I ask for feedback on why no one wants to be the first to speak in group settings. There is always a pregnant pause, and I get to say "There, see what I mean?" Why is that? I get responses (after prodding) that people are afraid that someone will think they're stupid or they talk funny or they might make a fool out of themselves or that they might say something that wasn't relevant or didn't make sense. It is why most of us dread public speaking.

So here's the cosmic joke: Everyone spends most of their waking hours worrying about what other people are thinking of them to the point that it drives what they say (or don't), where they work, where they live, who they live with, the car they drive, the way they dress—I mean, just about EVERYTHING! So, if all we are ever doing is obsessing about what other people are thinking of us, well then, no one is thinking about us! They're only thinking about what you are thinking of them! *We're all worrying about something no one is doing!* Think about that for a second. It's pretty ironic.

Oh sure, we might spend the first ten seconds or so sizing up a new acquaintance, but once we've "slotted their card" (made up our mind about what kind of person he/she is—a choice that's very hard to get people to do over) that's the last we think about the other person. From that point on, it's "I wonder what they're thinking about me?" Why do you think it's so hard to remember names? We aren't listening to the other person tell us their name. We're listening to ourselves worry about what we will say next so this new person won't think we're an idiot.

Overcome this, and you will be most of the way there in dealing with conflicts. It's our constant worry, even obsession, about what others are thinking of us, that derails our ability to connect with and guide people at a time when they have lost control and need leadership the most—when they are attacking us. When we are being verbally attacked, our attacker is NOT thinking about us.

They are thinking about what we must be thinking of them! That's often why they are attacking. They are seeking to change the way you are thinking about them (so they think). We'll talk more about that in a little while.

That's a complicated joke but if you'll read it over a few times and think about it for a while, you'll see just how much conflict is caused by this basic flaw in our thinking—the Cosmic Joke.

Cornerstone #4
Right to Harm vs. Right to Choose

One of the fundamental differences between Aikido and other highly popular martial arts such as Tae Kwon Do, Kung Fu and Karate is a belief in the "Right to Harm." The majority of martial arts operate on the premise that, because someone is attacking us and intends to do us harm, we have the right to injure, maim, and even kill our attacker. This is further perpetuated in action movies where right vanquishes wrong, usually with lots of blood, gore, and loss of life.

Aikido is based on the opposite premise that just because someone else is attacking us, we do not have the right to harm that person. It is unique in that instead of blocking a strike and striking back in an effort to overpower the attacker, Aikidoists learn how to blend with the incoming energy of the attacker in such a way that the energy is redirected and diffused. The situation is resolved without injury to the attacker or the attacked. *Stay CALM* explores this powerful concept in great detail.

Aikido's founder, Morihei Ueshiba, developed this concept of harmonization after years of practice in many forms of martial arts and meditation. Just recently, new discoveries about how the brain functions under the influence of anger provided stunning evidence that having the ability to blend with an attack is the correct scientific solution as well. Research into the relatively new field of Emotional Intelligence (known as "EQ"), pioneered by expert Daniel Goleman, has been detailed in his most recent book *Primal Leadership*.

In this work, Goleman explains how a part of our ancient primal brain (the amygdala) can take command of and hijack the decision-making part of our brain (the neocortex) when fear or anger come into play.

The amygdala, a walnut-sized lobe in the center of our brain, is the source of intuition that has kept *Homo sapiens* alive throughout human evolution. However, it is also the part that makes it impossible to reason with someone whose decision-making ability is disabled by the flood of adrenaline that is dumped into the bloodstream on command by the amygdala. This makes reasoning with someone who is attacking you as useless as trying to reason with someone who is drunk.

This fourth cornerstone is critical in building the solid foundation from which to respond to a verbal (or physical) attack: YOU MUST CHOOSE! The attacker has temporarily lost the ability to use the prefrontal lobe to make decisions. He cannot access that part of his brain, so you must make the choices he cannot until he regains access

and can reason again. The reward is that when you choose, you earn the right to guide instead of harm, to lead instead of becoming a victim.

Together, these cornerstones will provide you with a new "operating system" that will let you see verbal attackers as people who really want and need to be understood and to feel important. These are people who, because of their own internal dialogue, have temporarily lost control of their ability to use reason and logic and instead resort to violence, either verbal or physical.

A Platform of Compassion

A Platform of Compassion

You are now ready to construct a Platform of Compassion based upon these Four Cornerstones of Human Interaction. I suggest you make a copy of this page and keep it handy until you have these principles locked into your conscious mind:

Cornerstone #1: **What Everybody Wants** **To Feel Important and Be Understood**	Cornerstone #2: **The Internal Dialogue** **It's OK to Talk Nice to Yourself**
Make certain people can tell that you want to understand them, and provide evidence that you realize the importance of what they do and who they are, just as they are. This cornerstone alone can make all the difference in your ability to communicate with better results.	How we talk to ourselves has tremendous influence on the way we talk to others. More importantly, the way we hear others is often a reflection of the way we talk to ourselves. This can lead to assumptions and judgment—the root of all conflict.
Cornerstone #3: **The Cosmic Joke** **What Others Think of Me Is None of My Business**	Cornerstone #4: **Right to Harm vs. Right to Choose** **You Get to Choose**
Everyone is scared silly of what other people are thinking of them; it's all we think about. If all anyone is worrying about is what other people are thinking of them, then no one is thinking about YOU!!! We're all worried about something no one is doing!	When someone has been hijacked by their amygdala and has temporarily lost their ability to make decisions, we must remain in control of our own brain and guide them to regain their ability to reason. We do not have the inherent right to insult, injure or maim someone who is attacking us.

A Platform of Compassion

This is the foundation from which you will be most effective in responding to verbal attacks. Responding to a verbal attack with anything less than compassion (and compassion will be close to automatic if you have the Four Cornerstones in place) will nearly always trigger an even stronger response from your would-be opponent. When people are under the spell of an amygdala hijacking, they will instinctively ramp up their aggressions if they detect condescending or sarcastic vocal intonations or sense disdain and judgment in your body language and facial expression.

It is common to lose self-control as a result of Cornerstone #2—the Internal Dialogue not being fully understood. This is the most common breakdown in staying CALM. We see someone else who is acting out of control and we think to ourselves, "If I were acting that way I'd be really disappointed with myself; I might even hate myself. I'd *never* do anything like that!" This thinking is often at a sub-language level so you may not hear yourself having this thought, but it's there.

Even in less combative situations, we all judge other people using internal dialogue that goes something like this: "This guy is rolling his eyes and looks like he's falling asleep. He must be bored and thinks I'm a loser, 'cause if I were doing that it would be because I was bored and wishing the other person would just shut up."

Now we have an assumption about what this person said or did that may be entirely false. And here's the saying: *Assuming is the mother of all mess-ups!*

Please pay attention to your Internal Dialogue. Your self-talk is your own greatest enemy. Fortunately, it can also become your own best friend.

Fight or Flight

Unfortunately, the model of human being that we all use on our journey through life comes stock from the factory with only two default settings for dealing with attacks of any kind:

- Fight: block the attack and then attack back in the hopes that our retaliation will finish off the attacker before they finish us off
- Flight: turn tail and run (or freeze, clam up)

This is the basis of all combative martial arts: The attacker strikes; we block and counter strike; they block and counter our counter, etc., etc. You've seen it a million times if you've seen even one Bruce Lee or Jackie Chan movie. The reason that this type of martial art (or alternatively, becoming conflict averse, and just running away from attackers) is so popular is because it is more instinctive.

Verbally, this default looks like we're suppressing our feelings of hurt or betrayal—in essence mentally running from dealing with a verbal confrontation. We get into heated arguments where, *even if we win the argument, we've still lost.* We have lost our composure, our opportunity to deal constructively with a potentially destructive situation and, most importantly, we have lost our ability to guide and create real and lasting solutions. Thankfully there is an alternative to our caveman brain's "fight or flight" instinct.

No-Mind

No-Mind is an "add-on software option" for dealing with conflict that was refined to the highest level by the Japanese Samurai during the Edo Period from the early 1600's to the end of the 19th century. Called *mushin* by the Samurai, it is a state of relaxed focus and calm alertness that the Apache Indians referred to as being prepared for anything, expecting nothing.

In this state of no-mind, we are not putting out any messages or sending any signals, verbal or otherwise. We are only taking in information from as many sources and senses as possible, including our intuition. There is no judgment or reacting, only the calm and steady awareness of the incoming data.

We are in a state of No-Mind when there is no attachment to the outcome of the exchange. It is from this place that we can truly blend with our attacker, neutralize their attack, and guide them to partner with us to discover a new solution together.

The key to No-Mind is having no attachment to the outcome of any conflict situation. This does not mean being mindless or indifferent; rather, it is a state of mindful detachment. Being unattached allows you to connect with the other person or people involved without being trapped by your own unmovable position. Think of the willow tree: flexible enough to withstand the highest winds by bending without breaking.

A Platform of Compassion

Let's look more closely at Aikido to understand No-Mind in a physical application.

Aikido—Turning Discord into Harmony

What we resist, persists.
This is part of human nature. Watch little kids play fighting and you'll see one of them grab hold of another's wrist and the two will begin a tug of war in the attempt to regain control. It's how we're wired.

The founder of Aikido, Morihei Ueshiba (known as O Sensei or great teacher), said, "He who has won by force, has won but half the battle." To further that concept he also stated: "Victory over self is the only true victory." *In essence and in practice, Aikido is about learning how not to fight.*

It provides a third option to our instinctive "fight or flight" response when someone loses control and verbally attacks you. Let's call that option "Harmonize." Just as when the musicians in a jazz band seem to be playing independently from one another, then miraculously make the discordant sounds blend into beautiful sounds, we can learn to create harmony out of discordant dialogue.

The word Aikido roughly translates to "the way of the harmonious spirit" and it is the name O Sensei gave to the art that came to him in a vision where budo, or the art of war, became the way of love and harmony.

As a martial art, Aikido is purely defensive, but in a highly proactive way. "Self Defense" is a phrase that

A Platform of Compassion

conjures up images of subduing someone with some kind of magical technique or fancy hold. And to a first timer, parts of Aikido look just like that's what's happening. On closer inspection, we see that there is more to this martial art than meets the eye.

There are dozens of good books that explain the art of Aikido in detail, a few of which are listed in the recommended reading in the appendix. We will touch on the martial side of the art simply to provide a foundation for the principles of harmonizing with an attack.

The "Flip-Art" on the back of these pages can be viewed by thumbing the pages quickly and smoothly with your left hand, from back to front, to see "movies" of an Aikido response to an attack.

In this sequence, we see that the attacker is trying to force the attacked to go with him. Both parties are committed to their respective positions. The verbal equivalent might be something like this scenario: her boss telling her on Thursday afternoon that she must come to work on Saturday, and she already has plans. The boss wants her to come to his position, his way of thinking, while she is committed to her position, her way.

Two things stand out in the beginning frames of the Flip Art sequence. One, there is resistance—the attacker wants the attacked to come with him, the attacked does not wish to go, and the dynamic tension is evident at the point of contact on the wrist of the person being attacked. Two, the only thing the attacker is really controlling is the wrist of the attacked.

A Platform of Compassion

Relating this to our story, the only thing the boss really has control over is the issue around Saturday's work schedule. If that is the point of focus, the situation is likely to either escalate, resulting in a major conflict (she loses) or the boss gets his way, wins and she still loses, wrecking her Saturday plans.

As you can see in the Flip Art, the person who is being attacked can still move the rest of her body and turns to face the same direction as her attacker. In doing so she earns the right to guide the attacker to seeing different options and can replace tension with harmony. Let's define the turning point.

Tenkan—A Turning Point

Watching the Flip-Art we see the person being attacked leaving the attacked portion of her body, the wrist, in place while she moves her body to a different vantage point. That new position is standing right next to the attacker, facing the same direction as the attacker. This blending maneuver results in the attack being neutralized. Because there is no resistance, there is no longer a "fight."

In our Saturday work saga, she might say to the boss something like (and please finish the book before running out and "trying out this line"): "Wow, it sounds like we're really backed up in order processing and you need some help." It is natural to focus on the positions—her boss wants her to work on short notice, she has plans—and the point of contact: Saturday. Instead, she has shown the boss

A Platform of Compassion

that she is attempting to understand his position, and to see the situation the way he sees it.

This move is called "Tenkan," a Japanese word that in this context means "to turn and face the way your enemy is facing."

> Hot Tip: Lock this word in as an "anchor" and you will find it helps you access this method when conflict or resistance occurs. Just imagine yourself meeting with verbal resistance and say "Tenkan" over and over again so you will have a programmed trigger for dealing with the conflict.

The boss in our example is known for his poor tactical planning and has consistently put burdens on his people by scheduling additional hours at the last minute. By stating what she imagines his situation to be—orders that need to be processed before Monday—he is placed in a non–threatening, neutral situation. Obviously, the boss is accustomed to people resisting his requests for last minute scheduling nightmares and was prepared to combat that resistance.

The employee might continue from that neutral place. For example, she could request that they look together at options for getting the orders entered before the end of business on Friday, either by working late or coming in early, finding some other staff members to help level the load, or whatever makes sense in the situation.

Remember, the attacker (or in this example, the

A Platform of Compassion

instigator) is not in complete control of his decision-making ability. His initial attack or unreasonable request was launched or delivered based on his own subconscious behavior patterns. Because the person being confronted remained calm, she was able to choose to blend with and neutralize the situation. This choice earned the person being attacked the right to guide the instigator to a place where neither would be seriously harmed (or insulted). As a result, a more agreeable third option could be created, resulting in both parties getting what they wanted without disrupting the harmony of their professional relationship. We'll explore this in detail in the chapters to follow.

Reflecting on Our Foundation

We have covered a lot of ground in this chapter. Here's a summary of the Four Cornerstones of Human Interaction:

1) **What Everyone Wants**—We all want to feel important and be understood. Make certain people can tell that you want to understand them, and provide evidence that you realize the importance of what they do and who they are, just as they are.

2) **The Internal Dialogue**—The way we talk to ourselves has tremendous influence on the way we talk to others. More importantly, how we hear others is often a

reflection of how we talk to ourselves. This can lead to assumptions and judgment—the root of all conflict.

3) *The Cosmic Joke*—Everyone is scared silly of what other people are thinking of them. First of all, as Reverend Terry Cole-Whitaker says, "What other people think of me is none of my business," and second of all, if everyone is worrying about what other people are thinking of them, then no one is thinking about YOU!!! We're all worried about something no one is doing!

4) *Right to Harm vs. Right to Choose*—When someone has been hijacked by their amygdala and has temporarily lost their ability to make decisions, we must remain in control of our own neocortex and guide them to regain their ability to reason. We do not have the inherent right to insult, injure, or abuse someone who is attacking us.

We built a Platform of Compassion by installing a third option on the drop-down menu that appears when we are faced with any sort of confrontation. That option is "Harmonize," which offers us something besides the original equipment choices of "Fight" or "Flight" that come hardwired into these human bodies we are using to explore time and space.

We learned that one of the ways to achieve harmony when under attack is to maintain a state called No-Mind when faced with conflict. This does not mean "mindless"

A Platform of Compassion

but rather a detached state of mindfulness. No-Mind allows us to take in all information, including intuition, without passing judgment on, or assigning meaning to someone who has lost self-control and is attacking us.

And we talked about Aikido, the way of the harmonious spirit. This martial art teaches us to look for the most harmonious way to blend with any situation, including violence, and neutralize the attack, earning the attacked the right to guide the attacker to a place of resolve.

The anchor word we learned to help us key into the *Stay CALM Method*™ is Tenkan, a Japanese word that, for this method, means "turn and see things from your attacker's point of view."

The cement that holds the platform together is compassion. You must truly want to protect people from harm. Without this compassion, the method will be reduced to techniques, and techniques used to control others can backfire, often creating negative results.

Human Behavior

This chapter provides a personality profile system that will give you a general description of the different styles of behavior that are dominant in most people. It is a simple-to-remember system, one that you can use as a starting point to help you achieve a better understanding of the different types of people you deal with on a day-to-day basis. Best of all, once you have seen how the system is laid out, we will correlate it with the Four Cornerstones of Human Interaction and the Platform of Compassion you have just built in chapter one. This will complete the structure and format of the *Stay CALM Method*™.

As with most personality profile systems, there will be many similarities to other systems you might have seen. Feel free to blend what you already know into this system. The real advantage of the *Stay CALM* profile is that it is very easy to recall even under pressure. This is the moment when you really need to understand the person or people you are dealing with so you will be better able to connect and empathize with others to achieve a state of neutrality.

You may want to have some note paper available for this section as there will be several opportunities for self-evaluation and reflection.

Experience the following exercise with an open mind. Once you understand the question, go with your first impression as the best possible answer. This is an intuitive Whole Brain exercise, not a "Left Brain" analytical or "Right Brain" creative exercise. If you have not answered the question in less than five seconds, you are engaging in too much evaluation. Don't think about it, simply respond from intuition.

Please look at the four shapes below and mark down on a separate sheet of paper which shape you feel best represents you.

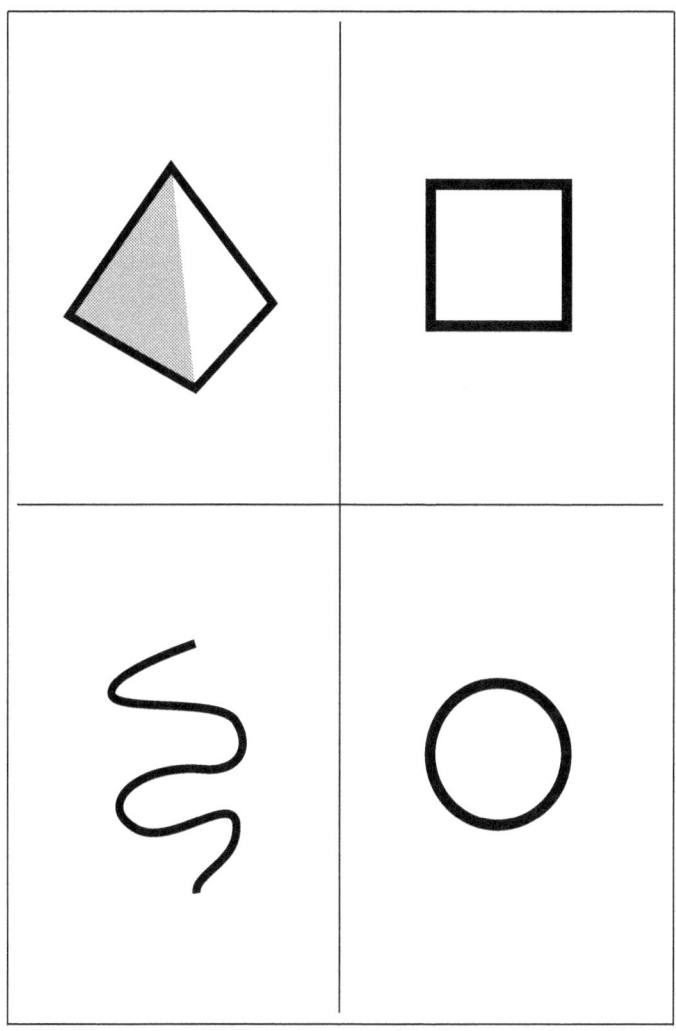

These shapes all relate to behavior styles. The shape you selected may very well tell about some of your dominant behavior characteristics. Keep in mind, this is not "who you are" but simply "how you behave." Most of us share traits with neighboring styles, rarely with diagonally opposed styles.

Below are the names and general behaviors of these four personality types.

Four Behavioral Styles

 **Controller**	**Analyst**
These are goal-oriented people who are often in positions of authority—executives, presidents, directors—with charisma and power.	These are data-driven people who are often in positions of research and design—engineers, IT staff, scientists. They are introverted and shy.
They have a strong need to be the final decision maker.	They have a strong need NOT to be wrong.
Relate your communication to their goals for best results.	Give them data, with deadlines for decisions, for best results.
 **Promoter**	**Supporter**
These are "Life is a Party" people who are often in positions related to sales and marketing. They are exuberant, outgoing, fun-lovers.	These are the caregivers of the world. Nurturing and helpful, to a fault, they are likely to be in customer support, nursing, or running a non-profit organization.
They have a strong need to be the center of attention.	They have a strong need to be liked.
Connect to and harness their creative energy for best results.	Be empathetic for best results.

The Formal/Informal and Dominant/Easy-Going lines are axes that we will define to further clarify these different personality types. They describe a continuum that we are always moving through, not finite points by which to judge others.

Understanding these axes will make it easier for you to connect with others right where they are and not where *you* think they "ought" to be.

Behavioral Styles Quadrant

Formal

The pyramid is the symbol of ultimate legacy. These are world-changers who are most comfortable in a tailored business suit, sitting in an immaculate office. Controllers are not comfortable with time-wasters such as listening to their significant other or just playing with the kids. "What is our agenda and how will it help me with my goals?" they ask.

They may not have a strong sense of fashion but if you need something edited, give it to a square. After all, what are the first four letters of Analyst? Every detail, including ones that probably don't matter much, are noted and brought into conversations that can sometimes feel a little like entering a time warp. "I need more data before I can make a decision," they say.

Dominant | **Easy-Going**

Our squiggly line defines promoters. They are outgoing and make friendly, easy, laughter-filled conversation. They will be the primary driver in any conversation, argument, relationship, or work/home environment. Positive or negative, it doesn't matter, as long as they're getting attention. "Can't we just figure it out when we get there?" they ask.

X's are kisses and O's are hugs right? These are the huggers, the good listeners, the supportive folks. Comfortable shoes, beds that go unmade and slightly late tax returns, all characterize circles. Voted most likely to become a doormat if they don't learn to say no. "Is there something I said that upset you?" they ask.

Informal

Here is the visual layout for the Four Cornerstones in their proper positions. This shows how the Four Behavioral Styles line up with the Four Cornerstones. Keep these top-level concerns in mind in stressful situations. This will help you deal with different behavioral styles.

Four Cornerstones and Four Behavioral Styles Alignment

Cornerstone #1: What Everybody Wants **To Feel Important and Be Understood**	Cornerstone #2: The Internal Dialogue **It's OK to Talk Nice to Yourself**
For the Controller, recognizing their important contributions, and understanding how critical their goals are, is a top priority. Making sure this cornerstone is addressed when dealing with Pyramid Style behaviors is strongly advised.	For the Analyst, the internal dialogue is extra powerful. And the fear of being wrong can make for an even more volatile condition. When dealing with a Square Style, try to smooth out all the hard edges and avoid judgments.
Cornerstone #3: The Cosmic Joke **What Others Think of Me Is None of My Business**	Cornerstone #4: Right to Harm vs. Right to Choose ***You* Get to Choose**
For the Promoter, one reason for their sometimes outlandish behavior is to cover up the overwhelming fear of what others are thinking of them. Put Squiggly Liners at ease by letting them know that they are OK just as they are.	For the Supporter, this choice is easy when things are going well. If you wind up on the bad side of a Supporter though, they can be cutting with their remarks. Dealing with upset Circle Styles means you must be the one to choose. Remain caring and compassionate to resolve the conflict.

Human Behavior

Tenkan, the art of turning and seeing things from our opponent's point of view is enhanced by understanding the Four Behavioral Styles and how they relate to the Four Cornerstones of Human Interaction.

This is pure strategy and spending time studying these scenarios will make the method that much easier to use when you are faced with an attack from one of the diagonally opposed behavior styles.

Controllers can bring calm back to a conflict situation with Supporters by turning and making a sincere effort to understand what their internal dialogue sounds like. Listening without criticizing will make the Supporter feel liked and stabilize the event.

Controllers attack Supporters using a tone of condescension, which can be devastating. Turn and look at The Cosmic Joke with the Controller and let them know you do care about their goals. They may be thinking you were being selfish and NOT thinking of them . . . Stay connected to them!

Analysts who instigate conflict do so from a place of stubborn inflexibility. For a Promoter this is foreign territory since innovative solutions (based on limited data) are always at the ready. Dealing with this covert type of attack requires getting into the Analyst's head and not making them wrong.

Analysts who are attacked by Promoters will be able to bring resolution to the matter when they are able to focus the Promoter on what makes that person feel important (themselves) and strive to understand them without a trace of condemnation or a condescending tone.

Human Behavior

As a final note, it should be pointed out that many of us shift our behavior styles to match our environment, with one style dominant at work and another at home. We may even switch from one style to another to match with different types of people that we interface with every day. So these behavior styles are not who we are but rather how we tend to behave, based on circumstance and our own point of view.

Ultimately, the "Apex" of human behavior is to stand at the apex of the two axes, without any attachment to our own dominant behavior style, and blend seamlessly with the behavior styles of those with whom we are communicating.

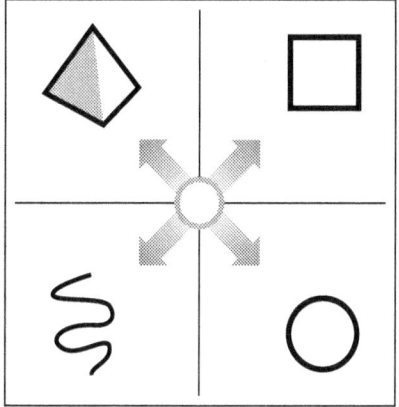

We are better prepared to deal with an attack by studying and becoming familiar with these personality characteristics and some typical conflict scenarios that occur between the different types. When we understand the behaviors of the personality types attacking us, we can use Tenkan more effectively to turn and really see the situation from our attacker's point of view.

Laying the Four Cornerstones of Human Interaction over the Behavioral Styles Quadrant gives us a broad view of human behavior that is simple to remember even under stress. Studying and becoming familiar with these tools

will enable us to relate more effectively with a wider spectrum of people and stay calm when facing a verbal attack.

Reflecting on Human Behavior

This chapter is an important one because it provides a simple, easy-to-use template to quickly determine the dominant behavior style of another person, even under pressure.

We identified these four personality types symbolized by a shape and contained in four quadrants:

Pyramid = Controller: World Changers—Strong charisma and goal oriented
Square = Analyst: Data Managers—Detail focused, researchers who are slow to decide
Squiggly Line = Promoter: Life of the Party—Creative energy, natural marketers
Circle = Supporter: Caregivers—Friend to the world, great customer service and everyone is a customer

Complementing this is a continuum between formal and informal behavior styles as well as between dominant and easy-going styles.

We explored the dynamic around conflict occurring between diagonally opposed personality types, and looked at strategies for using the Platform of Compassion when dealing with attacks from those who have Behavior Styles opposed to our own.

Finally, we discussed the fact that these styles are not who we are but rather how we tend to behave.

The Method

The Method

I am going to tap into some great minds to help with understanding the functional side of the *Stay CALM Method*™. One of the most well known people of all time in the art of Verbal Aikido, or seeing things from the other person's perspective, is a fellow by the name of Dale Carnegie. He wrote a book, first published in 1937, titled *How to Win Friends and Influence People*. It is alleged to have been reprinted more than any other book except the Bible.

In his book he explains, through fascinating stories, powerful principles for relating more effectively with other people. The principles are timeless, and the stories, though dated, are just as relevant today as when they were written some seven decades ago.

Principle #8 in Mr. Carnegie's book is: *Try honestly to see things from the other person's point of view.*

In the opening of the chapter that highlights this principle he says, "Remember that other people may be totally wrong. But they don't think so. Don't condemn them. Any fool can do that. Try to understand them. Only wise, tolerant, exceptional people even *try* to do that."

At the end of the chapter he tells us that if we only take one thing from reading the entire book, it should be that this principle may prove to be one of the major stepping stones of our entire career.

I find it interesting to note that Dale Carnegie's influence on the world began at much the same time as Morihei Ueshiba's. They were approaching the same issues—interpersonal relationships—at the same time and in much the

same way. The main difference was that Dale Carnegie was addressing verbal conflicts and O Sensei physical conflicts.

But there are other significant differences, namely the philosophical differences between Eastern and Western thought. Westerners, by and large, believe that if we change our minds, our bodies will follow. Thinking of life in a different way will, in time, have us acting differently.

In the East, the philosophy is the opposite. By engaging the body in different actions and practicing those physical movements until they are perfected, the mind will be perfected as well. And our thoughts will become more harmonious as a result of striving for harmony in our physical movements.

Personally, I have been engaged thoroughly in both schools of thought/action for many years and have discovered that both philosophies produce powerful results. And when the two are practiced simultaneously, they are exponentially more effective.

In the book, *Getting to Yes*, by Fisher, Ury, and Patton, we learn that people with opposing positions often share a common principle. This underlying principle ties the two parties together. When one person chooses to detach for a moment from their position and move to discuss the situation from the neutral basis of the shared principle, that person now has the ability to guide both people to discover a mutually beneficial solution, which was invisible when both parties were fighting for their position.

As we begin exploring attack scenarios, we will refer often to the unifying principle that, when focused on in

the guide stage, will help attackers recover their self control very quickly, preventing the typical escalation that normally occurs when people become married to their positions.

Graphically this concept can be illustrated as follows:

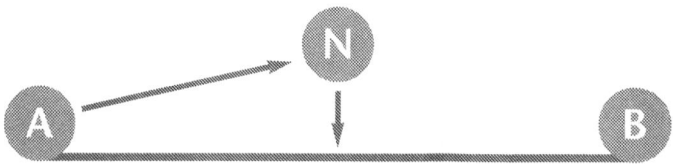

Person A and Person B have differing positions along a continuum of shared principle. Person A chooses to temporarily leave his position and goes to the neutral place above the different positions. From this vantage point, Person A is able to speak to the principle that unites their two positions. This gives Person A the chance to discover alternate options that could resolve the issue to satisfy both parties, options not visible from either position A or B.

Another amazing author and speaker, with terrific language explaining this philosophy, is Stephen Covey. In his landmark book, *The 7 Habits of Highly Effective People*, Mr. Covey offers Habit #5: "Seek First to Understand, Then to be Understood."

He says this is the single most important principle in the field of interpersonal relations. This habit is created by developing the skill of listening empathically. This means you listen with your heart, as well as your head, and make the sincere effort to really understand the situation from the perspective of the other person. What the other person hears (even if you say nothing) when you listen "reflectively"

is that you really "get" them—not only the picture they have in their mind's eye, but also the feelings they have in their hearts.

Here are two of the most powerful paragraphs in that chapter:

If you really seek to understand, without hypocrisy and without guile, there will be times when you will be literally stunned with the pure knowledge and understanding that will flow from you to another human being. It isn't even always necessary to talk in order to empathize.

In fact, sometimes words may just get in your way. That's one very important reason why technique alone will not work. [This] kind of understanding transcends technique. Isolated technique only gets in the way.

Covey warns that, if you are not sincere, don't even try these techniques. Doing so simply to manipulate or control others can create an openness and vulnerability that later may turn to harm when the other person discovers that you really *didn't* care, really didn't *want* to listen. As Covey says, ". . . techniques, the tip of the iceberg, have to come out of the massive base of character underneath."

In learning to recognize verbal attacks and crafting some sample responses, we will depend heavily on the impeccable research into verbal attacks and responses that Suzette Haden Elgin, Ph.D., teaches in her series of books published during the 80's under the franchise of *The Gentle Art of Verbal Self-Defense*.

The Method

To show how well aligned the *Stay CALM Method*™ is with Dr. Elgin's work, I'll excerpt this from the introduction to her inaugural edition published in 1980:

> *Unlike a number of books now available, [this book] is not intended to train you to attack others or to be violent yourself. Instead you will learn how to use your opponent's strength and momentum as tools for your own defense. You will learn to head off verbal confrontation so skillfully that it rarely happens, and to do so with honor. The person with a black belt in a martial art is not likely to be a violent person. Knowing that you are fully capable not only of defending yourself adequately, but also of inflicting harm on others, makes you a very careful person. Far more careful than you would be if you reacted to every threatening situation with an untrained panic response.*

In developing the new skills needed to communicate with better results, it is important that you have a partner or two with whom you can practice both the action side and the verbal techniques of the *Stay CALM Method*™ so that you can apply the method easily in times of stress.

By understanding the feeling of Tenkan, and practicing staying calm even when someone is grabbing you and trying to take you over to their way of thinking, you will be well equipped to maintain a state of No-Mind and perform Tenkan even under the stress of a conflict.

In fact, without practice, this and all the other books I've mentioned will be just more "Shelf Help" books, a

The Method

phrase I heard in the PSI Seminars personal development program I refer to in the appendix. One of the facilitators, Jeff Rogers, discussed alleged self-help books that get read and then shelved with no new experiences or action occurring in the reader's life, thus no new or different results. But they look good on the shelf.

So find a partner and practice the movement you see in the Flip Art on the back of these pages. Your partner reaches across as if to shake your hand but instead grasps your wrist. Without grasping back, try pulling away from your grasping partner to create some resistance. Don't go crazy and start a tug of war, but encourage your partner to apply enough pull so you feel you need to pull back. Then, leaving your grasped wrist right where it is in space, step up right beside your partner and face the same direction as he, looking together at your grasped wrist.

Notice how the fight ends as soon as you do this. In the moment you choose to blend with the attack, face the same direction as your attacker, and look *with* him at the area of resistance, the resistance disappears. It's uncanny and a little disorienting—definitely NOT what the attacker was expecting.

Often, the attacker will waver or stumble slightly, their balance being disrupted by this unexpected alignment of what was an opposing force just moments ago.

This alignment, which we'll call neutrality, **must** be achieved before it is possible to guide your attacker-turned-partner. Otherwise, it's still a fight. Our instinct

The Method

tells us to take a stand, to hold our position, to fight back. That is our caveman brain speaking.

From here on, the person who executed Tenkan has earned the right to guide the attacker. By putting his free hand on the side of the attacker's head, he is able to gently redirect his attention to another point of view, another way of seeing things.

Blend (Part One)

Blend (Part One)

ow let's begin exploring the functional side of CALM—Communicative Aikido Leadership Method—in responding to verbal attacks.

There are three steps to executing the *Stay CALM Method*™. They are:
1) **Blend**
2) **Neutralize**
3) **Guide**

The Blend Step is so totally counterintuitive that it will be the most challenging step to understand, adopt, and become comfortable executing. We're going to spend some time on this step to make sure it gets fully installed.

One of the reasons that blending is so difficult is because of Cornerstone #1: We all want to be understood. *We are so desperate to be understood that when we are attacked, we want to immediately correct the misunderstanding so we can recover this important psychological need.*

So instead of taking the time to blend and neutralize and earn the right to guide, we jump straight to the Guide Step in an effort to be understood ourselves. This only encourages the attacker to push or pull even harder.

What we resist will persist.

The reason I'm drilling this point into the ground (and hopefully into your subconscious) is that in a few pages, we're going to look at some of the language structures

that you would hear if you were observing a CALM practitioner blending with a verbal attack.

The risk is that you will take these language bits and memorize them thinking, "Now I'll be able to keep other people from hurting me just by saying these lines." Nothing could be further from the truth. Do not confuse the language of CALM for the lesson of CALM. Reread this section at least twice, read a few of the books that are referenced in this chapter, and find a partner to practice with, so when you face a verbal confrontation, you can *Stay CALM*. Don't just memorize these lines, thinking that will suffice.

Remember *Mad Magazine*'s "Snappy Answers to Stupid Questions"? You are likely to sound like that if you simply memorize the responses and ignore the core principles that this work represents.

Your words are secondary. You will say what needs to be said in the moment of the attack if you are committed to Tenkan, to turning and seeing things from your opponent's point of view. If you'll make the point of mentally stepping up, turning around and seeing the situation from the other person's perspective, no matter what you say, it will come from a place of wanting to partner with your would-be opponent, and discover a solution together.

Final Warning: You may find yourself reading these attack phrases and thinking to yourself in sentences that start with, "Yeah but they're wrong . . ." or "If they said that, I'd tell 'em . . ." If so, you are attempting to guide the attacker before you have blended. Go back and review the beginning of this chapter and come back to this section

with the intent to execute a true Tenkan. Not to say that you must agree with your attacker, but that you must see the situation the way they see it—without making them right or wrong—by simply observing, not evaluating.

The majority of overt, violent verbal attacks are the end result of escalating, covert attacks. It is important to know that many times, when people are verbally attacking you in a covert fashion, they may not be consciously aware of the fact that they are in the beginning stages of creating a conflict scenario. They are often playing out life scenarios that they have been modeling since childhood from the example of adults and are completely unaware of the feelings and unmet needs that are driving them to threaten or attack. These life scenarios are actually "stories" that people have concocted in their minds about what your actions must mean.

Human beings are meaning making machines. We observe a behavior, hear a particular string of words, or read something and in the flash of a shutting synapse, we make that action or message into a meaningful story that creates an emotional response. We then link this emotional response (driven by our assumed-true story) to the facts we observed, and make the entire string of observed facts and imagined story into our version of "Reality."

From here, it is only a small jump to conclusions that will have us taking action towards others as if the story were real, making derogatory comments, hinting at accusations and throwing snide remarks around, "just-as-if" the make-believe story had actually occurred. This becomes the starting point for many of the covert verbal attacks that we encounter.

Blend (Part One)

Like coming into a movie in the middle, we are missing key pieces of the plot that went on in our attacker's head, and we are just as confused and unsure as to why this person is behaving in this manner, as if we'd missed part of the story line. Because we did!

So as you find yourself encountering situations like those in the following sample attack patterns, begin analyzing the motives behind the attacks, as it will serve you well to be curious about the real story. In being curious, we are able to maintain an objective viewpoint and avoid being sucked into a story line we know nothing about.

Types of Verbal Attacks

One of the most critical components of the *Stay CALM Method*™ is the skill to recognize various types of verbal attacks. In the following examples I will use italics to indicate words or parts of words that get extra emphasis when they are part of an attack.

I must give much credit to Suzette Haden Elgin, Ph.D. She is a linguist specializing in verbal self defense, which she defines in a series of books written during the 80's starting with *The Gentle Art of Verbal Self-Defense*.

Dr. Elgin has proposed a set of structures she calls the "Verbal Attack Patterns" (VAP's) of the English language. My analysis of these attacks and my proposed responses differ from Dr. Elgin's in various ways, but I could not have developed them for the *Stay CALM Method*™ without the solid foundation she has provided. There are six patterns from that set that we will review in the *Stay CALM Method*™.

Blend (Part One)

1) "If you really (X), you would/wouldn't (Y) . . ."
2) "If you really (X) you wouldn't want to (Y) . . ."
3) "Don't you even care . . .?"
4) "Even a(n) (X) should (Y) . . ."
5) "Everyone understands why you (X) . . ."
6) "A person who (X) (Y) . . ."

I'm sure many of us can relate to hearing something like this from someone as young as six or seven:

"If you *really* loved me you'd buy me a computer like all the *other* kids have."

This is a classic verbal attack pattern that can be modified to fit nearly any environment. Again, the italicized words are those that get emphatic stress to create meaning beyond the actual words spoken.

If you really . . .
- were committed to this relationship you wouldn't . . .
- wanted to be promoted you'd . . .
- had the motivation to support our team you'd . . .
- wanted to lose weight you wouldn't . . .

And so on and so forth.

This simple, but camouflaged verbal attack is really pretty elementary but how many times have you or parents you know gone down this rocky road in response to that six-year-old's tactic?
Dad: Oh, come on Alex, not *all* the kids have computers.
Child: They do *too; you* just don't *want* to get me one.
Dad: Now, I know Mackenzie doesn't have one.

Blend (Part One)

Child: She does too, *up* in her *room*. You just don't know *anything*!
Dad: All right young man, that's enough out of you! You go to your room and stay there until you can act like a decent person.

Game, set, and match. The child goes running off crying and slams his bedroom door, but Dad's the loser in this one, having let the six-year-old get away with one of the most transparent yet easily missed verbal attack sequences in our culture.

The "If you really (X) then you would/wouldn't (Y)" attack is based on the fact that most of us, when faced with this linguistic sequence, often take the "bait" which is the (Y) in the attack. We miss entirely the child's hidden agenda, which we will call the presupposition (X), which preceded the bait. By ignoring the presupposition we admit, by default, that its premise is true.

When the child says, "If you really loved me you'd buy me a computer," the presupposition is that Dad doesn't really love him. Instead of finding out what that means, Dad takes the bait and unwittingly finds himself vindicating the child's presupposition. Not bad for a six-year-old.

In using the *Stay CALM Method*™, Dad would blend with the initial presupposition and ignore the bait entirely:

Child: If you *really* loved me you'd buy me a computer like all the *other* kids have.

Blend (Part One)

Dad: Wow, it sounds like you're thinking I don't love you. When did you start thinking that?
Child: When you called me a *knucklehead* in front of Uncle *Tommy, that's* when!

By blending with the child, Dad has successfully brought the real issue out in the open, can discuss this with his child, and work to resolve the upset with appropriate compassion and care.

Great. So we've gained some confidence in dealing with six-year-olds. What about the world of adults slinging more complex verbal daggers our way?

Ever hear something like this?

Manager: If you were *really* committed to this department, you wouldn't even *want* to turn these reports in looking like *this*.

O.K., now we're moving into a more complex and sophisticated attack. The presupposition is clear based on the previous attack pattern: "You aren't really committed to this department" but additional layers of presupposition have been added:

1) The report you turned in is less than satisfactory
2) You not only knew that, but intended to do a poor job.

This is tougher to blend with because the temptation to take the bait—the quality of the report—is so great that the topics of our commitment to the department and our

commitment to doing quality work are likely never to see the light of day.

Let's look at a possible blend sequence to turn this attack into a solution-oriented exchange between manager and employee (we will not go past the blend step here so be prepared for a cliff-hanger):

Manager: If you were *really* committed to this department, you wouldn't even *want* to turn these reports in looking like *this*.

Employee: It sounds like you're frustrated with me and need my commitment to our department. I want to satisfy your expectations for high quality. What exactly are you requesting of me?

Manager: I *am* frustrated. This report is missing the stats regarding turnover that I had specifically asked to be included in each weekly report.

This blend is handled well by the employee. The manager can tell that the employee is seeking to understand the way the manager is feeling and wants to find out exactly where the breakdown occurred.

By not taking the bait and becoming defensive, the employee has provided clear evidence that he or she is indeed committed to the department, and wants to provide complete reports that meet with the manager's expectations for quality.

So let's discuss the specifics of this blend sequence. The first component that must be in place is the employee

Blend (Part One)

maintaining control of his or her vocal intonations. Our instinct to defend can be so strong that in our attempt to discover the other person's perspective we can end up sounding sarcastic, condescending, or patronizing.

Try this: Say the employee's response to the manager's attack as a string of sarcastic comments and see if you can make your response into a counter-attack. Can you hear how ineffective this would be?

Then practice saying the employee's response with a sincere desire to empathize with the feelings of the other person and a very real attempt to discover the source of the actual problem. Can you say this with a level of compassion and empathy that *you* would respond to favorably if it were said to *you* that way?

Practicing these responses by using scenarios that you actually face in your life, especially on tape or using a digital recorder, will help immensely and prepare you for the next time you face a verbal attack.

In the last example, I made no effort to explain the rest of the sequence as to how the employee would guide the manager to understand his or her own perspective, or provide a reasonable solution for the breakdown.

This is because I want to provide examples of people moving from the attack to a place of neutrality by blending with their attackers. Once neutral ground is reached, the Guide Step will have a much better chance of producing favorable results.

One of the most powerful first responses to a verbal attack is to identify the feelings that our attacker might be

experiencing. When we make the effort to discover how our attacker is feeling, this short-circuits our attacker, starts to bring him back to a decision-making mode and helps him regain control over his prefrontal cortex. This heightens his ability to choose instead of reacting based on learned patterns of verbal abuse.

The father in the previous CALM example tuned into his son's feelings of not being loved and found a way to achieve neutrality. The employee confirmed that she had blended with the manager when the manager agreed that she was frustrated.

In the next chapter we will provide a helping hand in acquiring the skills exhibited by the dad and by the employee in the sample attack patterns we have discussed in Part One.

Once we have the tools for understanding our attacker's real feelings and unmet needs, we will return for Part Two of the Blend Step.

Real Feelings

Real Feelings

The challenge we face in connecting with the feelings of a verbal attacker is that many of us are so out of touch with our own feelings, trying to empathize with another's can be like trying to read ancient Egyptian hieroglyphics. We see the body language and hear the vocal intonations, but we struggle to determine what they all mean.

In this and the chapters to follow, I will share with you concepts from the work of another amazing author named Marshall B. Rosenberg, Ph.D. He compiled a list of feelings in his important book, *Nonviolent Communication: A Language of Life*.

People are always seeking to get their needs met. Abraham Maslow, a renowned psychologist of the 20th century, defined mankind's needs and organized them into a pyramid of importance as we progress through life. Once we have handled the basics in Maslow's hierarchy—water, food, shelter, etc.—we address higher level needs around family, status, community, legacy, and actualization. Depending on our level of self-awareness, we will have greater or lesser skills in expressing those needs and ensuring that we make honest and compassionate requests of others who can support us in fulfilling those needs.

To provide *Stay CALM* practitioners a meaningful list of feelings, I've included Dr. Rosenberg's list on the following pages to refer to in building your language of compassion.

Strive to add as many of these to your vocabulary as possible. It will prove to be an invaluable tool in assisting other people (and yourself) in being able to accurately identify feelings and determine needs that are or are not being fulfilled.

Real Feelings

How we are likely to feel when our needs *are* being met:

Absorbed	Engrossed	Perky
Affectionate	Enthusiastic	Pleasant
Alert	Excited	Pleased
Alive	Friendly	Proud
Amazed	Fulfilled	Quiet
Amused	Glad	Radiant
Appreciative	Gleeful	Refreshed
Aroused	Glowing	Relaxed
Astonished	Good-humored	Relieved
Blissful	Grateful	Satisfied
Breathless	Gratified	Secure
Buoyant	Happy	Sensitive
Calm	Hopeful	Serene
Carefree	Inquisitive	Spellbound
Cheerful	Inspired	Splendid
Complacent	Intense	Stimulated
Concerned	Interested	Surprised
Confident	Intrigued	Tender
Contented	Invigorated	Thankful
Cool	Involved	Thrilled
Curious	Joyous/Joyful	Touched
Dazzled	Loving	Tranquil
Delighted	Mellow	Trusting
Eager	Merry	Upbeat
Ecstatic	Moved	Warm
Elated	Optimistic	Wide-awake
Enchanted	Overjoyed	Wonderful
Encouraged	Overwhelmed	Youthful
Energetic	Peaceful	Zestful

Source: *Nonviolent Communication: A Language of Life*
© Marshall B. Rosenberg, 2003
Reprinted with permission of PuddleDancer Press

Real Feelings

How we are likely to feel when our needs are *not* being met:

Afraid	Disgusted	Lethargic
Aggravated	Disheartened	Lonely
Agitated	Dismayed	Mad
Alarmed	Displeased	Mean
Aloof	Distressed	Miserable
Angry	Disturbed	Mournful
Anguished	Downcast	Nervous
Annoyed	Dull	Numb
Anxious	Edgy	Overwhelmed
Apathetic	Embarrassed	Panicky
Apprehensive	Embittered	Passive
Aroused	Exhausted	Pessimistic
Ashamed	Fatigued	Reluctant
Beat	Fearful	Repelled
Bewildered	Frightened	Resentful
Bitter	Furious	Restless
Blah	Gloomy	Sad
Blue	Guilty	Scared
Bored	Harried	Sensitive
Brokenhearted	Heavy	Shocked
Cold	Helpless	Skeptical
Concerned	Hesitant	Sorrowful
Confused	Horrified	Suspicious
Cross	Horrible	Terrified
Dejected	Hostile	Troubled
Depressed	Hurt	Uncomfortable
Despairing	Impatient	Uneasy
Despondent	Indifferent	Unhappy
Detached	Intense	Unsteady
Disenchanted	Irate	Upset
Disappointed	Irritated	Uptight
Discouraged	Jealous	Withdrawn
Disgruntled	Lazy	Worried

Source: *Nonviolent Communication: A Language of Life*
© Marshall B. Rosenberg, 2003
Reprinted with permission of PuddleDancer Press

Blend (Part Two)

Blend (Part Two)

Dr. Rosenberg recommends separating *what* we observe from our *evaluation* of what we observe. He points out that for most of us, *it is difficult to make observations of people and their behavior that are free of judgment, criticism, or other forms of analysis.*

This is the ticket price to get into the game of communicating without being a victim of verbal abuse. Being able to simply acknowledge another person's position without making condemning remarks or holding a contemptuous attitude toward them is critical. It supports our ability to step off the line of attack, perform Tenkan, and guide our attacker to a satisfactory solution to the real issues underlying the attack.

As we delve further into various forms of attacks, we will become effective when we develop the ability to enter the state of No-Mind, simply observe, then make a connection with what the attacker is feeling as a result of not having his needs met.

Be observant of attackers who describe non-feelings using "feel" language. Some typical attacks and complaints that do not clearly express the speaker's true feelings might sound like these examples:

Wife: I feel as if I'm living with a zombie. You never talk to me or tell me about what's going on with you.

"Living with a zombie" is a non-feeling and when the word feel is followed by words such as *that, as if, like,* and *you,* she is only describing how she thinks or her evaluation of the situation, not how she feels.

Sister (to her brother): I feel it is useless to talk to my boyfriend; he simply refuses to listen.

More non-feeling language is evidenced when the word feel is followed by words such as *I, you, he, she, they,* and *it.*
Employee: I feel my boss is being manipulative; he plays all of us against each other.

Language referring to people or things indicates a lack of connection with the actual feelings and almost always indicates a judgment by the speaker.

When you hear people using this type of language, *make an effort to reflect back their lack of authentic expression by suggesting possible feelings for them to see if you can pinpoint their feelings and needs.*
Wife: I feel as if I'm living with a zombie. You never talk to me or tell me about what's going on with you.
Husband: It sounds like you're feeling neglected and even a little mad because you're not getting enough attention from me. Do you want to have more time to talk on a regular basis?

This stops the attack (which is subtle and masked as an accusation) dead in its tracks (zombie pun fully intended) by neutralizing the attacker, and allows for a real two-way conversation to begin.

It beats the heck out of, "You'd go into zombie mode too if you had to listen to yourself whining about your day and all the people who are out to get you." From this response, the husband will be in the doghouse, *again.*

Blend (Part Two)

Another typical attack pattern that Dr. Elgin exposes in *The Gentle Art of Verbal Self-Defense* is the classic "Don't you even care about (X)?"

(X) can be any number of juicy fillers:

... your grades?
... your health?
... your job?
... your children?

Doctor: Don't you even *care* about the harm your smoking is doing to the rest of your family, let alone to your *own* body?

The word "even" is a major flag warning you that you are being attacked. It puts the final touches on the last of these three presuppositions that are wrapped up in this attack:

1) You don't care about (X)
2) You *should* care about (X) and you're bad not to
3) Therefore, you should feel very guilty about this.

Performing Tenkan to blend with attacks of this type requires that we understand our attacker's true intent, which is to get us to shift our behaviors.

The way we are behaving now is not acceptable to them. They really want to accept us, but they won't if we are unable to meet their conditions.

Often these attacks are put forth by Pyramid Controllers or Square Analysts who are focused on accomplishing their

Blend (Part Two)

own goals, and can't understand why you won't take action on their recommendation.

A patient who could remain observational might be able to blend by dealing with this attack as follows:

Patient: Doctor, I get the sense that you're feeling concerned about my ability to overcome my addiction to smoking and sad that I'm possibly doing harm to my family. Are you willing to discuss this from the perspective that I do care about the people I love, and that I do want your help?

This response makes a clear request for a discussion free of presuppositions. The neutrality is clear and either party can take the guiding role in the dialogue to follow.

This is an attack pattern that is based on an unproved assumption that the patient doesn't care about his family. That assumption needs to be gently uncovered, and a request made that if the doctor and patient are to talk about this it will be best done without that assumption driving the dialogue.

In exposing the assumption without blame, most attackers regain their reasoning ability and will accommodate our request without continuing the attack. It must be done delicately and without a hint of blame or accusation in the response. Again, try to see things from the doctor's point of view, recognize the shared principle (gaining control over an unhealthy addiction) and seek to find a neutral place from which to begin an open dialogue.

Blend (Part Two)

The next attack pattern is far from subtle. It lands like a brick upside the head and if the person being attacked takes the bait, the consequences are equally painful. Here is the structure for this attack:

"Even (X) should (Y)."

An example would sound like this in an exchange between a college professor and a first year student:

Professor: Even someone *your* age should know that term papers *have* to be typed.

Presuppositions are as follows:
1) Whatever your age, there is something wrong with being that age; it's not an age to be proud of
2) The fact that term papers have to be typed is so well known that for you not to know it is further proof of how inferior you are
3) You should feel very guilty and ashamed

Naturally there are several small words that can go between (X) and (Y). These are words that, like "even," pack a large amount of information into a very small space:

Even (X) Should (Y)

Ought to	Could	Would
Might	Can	May
Must	Will	

Blend (Part Two)

And the filler for (X) and (Y) will sound pretty familiar:
Even *you* . . .
a *woman* . . .
a *seventh-grader* . . .
a *plumber* . . .
someone *your* age . . .
a high school *dropout* . . .
. . . **should** (or other small but powerful word) . . .
. . . be able to understand how cars work.
. . . be able to understand the basic facts of life.
. . . appreciate the fact that money doesn't grow on trees.
. . . know that term papers have to be typed.
. . . be able to keep a job for longer than two months.

A blend with this overt type of attack is fairly straightforward.

Professor: Even someone *your* age should know that term papers have to be typed.

Student: You seem upset and discouraged. Is that because you needed me to meet your expectations about the quality of my term paper?

Professor: Yes, that's right, and I am discouraged with you.

Student: I apologize for this. May I request that we talk about what my options are at this point?

Though it is a straightforward blend, there are some technical details that should be pointed out. First of all, this response includes a small portion of the Guide Step.

Blend (Part Two)

This is so you can begin to see where and how to guide an attacker once the neutral step has been achieved.

In this sample conversation the student was able to provide the professor with solid evidence that he was seeing the situation from the professor's point of view. As soon as it was clear that the professor was neutral, as evidenced by his agreement with the student's assessment of his feelings and the needs that were driving those feelings, the student could begin to guide.

At this point, without denying the professor, the student has indeed earned the right to make a request for a solutions-oriented discussion, and begin the process of guiding the professor in a conversation about options. The apology keeps the professor's ego intact.

The professor needed to have his importance confirmed and likely wanted to make sure the student was clear in his own goal of having only typed term papers to make the task of reading all of them much easier. The student will do well to confirm to the professor that he understands this rule and will do his utmost to be aware of and fulfill the professor's expectations.

Avoiding the entire presupposition around being old enough to know better, or being incompetent for his age, the student was able to quickly return the professor to having a dialogue instead of following the usual pattern of this attack.

Typical responses to this type of attack are to make excuses as to why the paper wasn't typed, to justify the paper as submitted, or make ridiculous claims about being

Blend (Part Two)

ignorant of the standards for term papers, all of which might inspire the professor to gain a feeling of importance by chastising the student.

A more complex and vicious attack pattern that we have all encountered at some point is this:

"Everyone understands why you (X)."

Here (X) might be any number of claims, such as you:
- ... are so emotional
- ... are so confused
- ... are so angry
- ... really haven't been yourself lately
- ... can't achieve your sales numbers
- ... are having so much trouble adjusting to (Y)

As an example:

Commanding Officer: Soldier, everyone in your unit understands why you are having so much trouble adjusting to your new duties.

This is a particularly troublesome attack pattern because it is often delivered in a tone of kindness and often from people in authority or positions of power who appear to be trying to help us. Feelings of confusion, betrayal, and resentment are common, making it difficult to blend with this attack.

Our instinct tells us to lash out and ask who in the unit is saying bad things about us, or deny angrily that we

Blend (Part Two)

are having any troubles adjusting, which only further corroborates the presuppositions.

Equally foolish is an attempt to argue that you can adjust to the duties, make the sales numbers, and not be emotional or whatever is alleged in (X) that you can't do. This is exactly what the attacker is expecting to encounter as a response.

This attack presupposes the following:
- There is something very wrong with you.
- This "something wrong" is well known to everyone around you.
- This "something wrong" is so wrong that we are all more than willing to forgive you for (X).
- You should be very, very grateful to all of us for being so perceptive and understanding.
- You should be very, very ashamed of yourself.

This attack pattern is based on a tried and true fundamental mechanism that is tied in with Cornerstone #3—The Cosmic Joke. We all have *something* we view as our "shameful little secret," and we would hate for anybody else to know about "IT!"

Anyone employing this attack pattern can count on *you* knowing what that secret is, even if *they* don't, and that you will likely react to "a person in your situation" or to "everyone understands why you (X)" with this thought: "Oh, no! Everybody knows about IT!"

Blend (Part Two)

Don't fall for this. Your attacker most likely doesn't really know about IT (and who cares if they do; we all have an "IT") and *they are trying to goad you into a counter-attack pattern that will unveil your weakness enabling them to further control and abuse you.*

This is a tricky attack and should be dealt with very carefully. There are many pitfalls in responding to this while attempting to maintain your own integrity.

Here is a possible response to this type of attack:

Commanding Officer: Soldier, everyone in your unit understands why you are having so much trouble adjusting to your new duties.

Soldier: (without blatant sarcasm) Sir, I appreciate that the unit has this much concern for me. Does this warrant a discussion with the entire group? I'm not sure what *you* would like to talk to me about.

This is a tough response, especially considering the circumstances, but the soldier is in a precarious position in that the CO has him cornered, alone, and is making claims about the unit's alleged issue with him.

This is not a pure blend maneuver in that the intent of the CO is not clear. In order to smoke out the real issue (instead of assuming that it is about IT) this approach could produce the real concern. At the very least it aligns with the CO's statement and reduces the effectiveness of the tactic by the soldier's willingness to discuss the issue with the rest of the unit present.

Blend (Part Two)

The exchange might continue like this:

Commanding Officer: No, Soldier. We won't need to bring the rest of the unit in on this. I just can't figure out why you aren't getting your duties accomplished to standard!

Soldier: Sir, are you discouraged by the lack of enthusiasm for the duties I have been assigned?

Commanding Officer: Very discouraged, and disappointed too. You have great potential and you're not showing me what you're made of. I think it's because you're homesick.

At this point neutrality has been achieved because the soldier got the CO to come clean on what *he* thought the problem was, giving the soldier the chance to confirm the CO's real feelings. Now the soldier has earned the right to make a request such as this:

Soldier: Sir, can you please tell me more about what exactly you are expecting of me and what your plans are for me?

This example shows how critical it is to stay calm even during a vicious attack like this. By remaining open to the CO's real needs, and wanting to find out what the CO was really requesting of him, the soldier took the chance to blend in two moves.

Again, I would like to point out that the real reason for the attack was that the CO wanted to see a change in the soldier's behaviors. Knowing this is why people attack us will enable us to quickly discover what behaviors the

Blend (Part Two)

attacker wants to see changed and attempt to understand why they want them changed. From that point, and ONLY from that point, will there be any opening for discussing options and alternatives, and explaining our own point of view with our attacker/partner.

In a less charged scenario, the exchange may be even easier, resulting in a blend in only one move:

Employer: Sue, everyone here understands why you are having so much trouble fitting into this environment. We really *do* understand.

Sue: That is so perceptive of them, and I appreciate you mentioning it.

Employer: Well . . . that's not really what I wanted to talk to you about.

Sue: Oh, sorry. Nothing like a misunderstanding to start off a conversation! Why don't we start over?

Again, this tactic enables Sue to smoke out the real issue without creating any hostility and without taking any of the bait being offered in the attack pattern. By saying, "Nothing like a misunderstanding . . ." there was no blame assigned for the misunderstanding, and neutrality is gained immediately.

This is a language technique and will be very difficult to remember if you are attacked with this pattern. If you find yourself dealing with attacks of this nature, practice with a partner until you can do it with ease. Additionally, it may be that your internal dialogue and a habit of worrying about what others are thinking is showing up in

Blend (Part Two)

your facial expressions, body language, and vocal intonations. These are often the initial catalyst for people making this type of attack on you.

This explanation makes kids go "eeewww!" But it's a fact. When we speak, our vocal chords make the air molecules around us vibrate. Those vibrations are picked up by the receiver's eardrums. When we speak, we are literally touching another person's eardrums with our vocal chords, using air as the medium. How is your touch? Is it light and pleasant? Gruff and sarcastic? Straightforward and clear? Arrogant and self-righteous?

Think of it as physical touch and ask yourself, would you enjoy being touched the way you sound? If your voice has a shove or a grab in it, people will feel attacked no matter what your message might be.

Try recording yourself in regular conversation. Have a friend over and pick a few charged topics for discussion. Record for at least a half hour so you can get past being self-conscious about the recording. Then play this back and confirm with your friend that the recording is an accurate reproduction of the way your voice sounds. If so, then objectively listen to yourself speaking (this might be a bit of a shock to you. We are often dismayed that we don't sound to others the way we think we sound).

This is a sure-fire way to uncover vocal patterns and qualities that are annoying, or sound condescending, nervous, or whiney and is a great starting point towards making corrections in the way we modulate our voice.

Blend (Part Two)

Let's look at one last attack pattern that requires a language technique. Once handled, we will move into the last step of the *Stay CALM Method™*: The Guide.

The attack looks like this:
"A person who (X) (Y)."

The need to remain calm and detached from the outcome of this exchange is at an all-time high. This attack is designed to enable the attacker to single you out as that person who (X) and blame you for (Y). Implicit in the attack is that something bad is going to occur if you don't change your behaviors. The beauty of this attack is that the attacker is able to remain in Controller or Analyst mode by not directly referring to you.

The bait is so tempting. We instinctively jump for it and argue that we are not (X) and that we can handle (Y)! This is exactly what the attacker is planning on for your response.

Here's a sample exchange (poorly handled):

Manager: A person with serious emotional problems cannot possibly be expected to deal with the constant pressure and tension in this particular department.

Rick: How dare you insinuate that I have serious emotional problems! I've been tolerating the stress and tension of this department for six months without as much as a vacation! You have the nerve to tell me I've got emotional problems!? I'll tell you what I've got a problem with—your management style!

Blend (Part Two)

If you've seen the movie *Office Space*, you'll be reminded of the engineer that screams "Dammit, I've got people skills; don't you idiots understand that?" at the two consultants who are trying to figure out what exactly this engineer does.

Don't take the bait. It is not necessary to make any attempt to communicate meaningfully with someone who is hiding behind this type of attack. Call them out from behind their pretense and get them to say what they actually mean to say. Then you can blend. For now, try a response that goes like so:

Manager: A person with serious emotional problems cannot possibly be expected to deal with the constant pressure and tension in this particular department.

Rick: I couldn't agree with you more. The problem is, of course, deciding how a situation of this kind should be dealt with.

(NOTE: The person who speaks first after this statement will *lose* the right to guide. Rick should keep quiet, no matter how pregnant the pause on the part of Manager)

Manager (fishing, after 12 awkward seconds): Well . . . Rick . . . what do you think ought to be the first step?

Rick: Problems of this type are outside my expertise. I'd probably suggest bringing in an outside expert if none can be found on our staff.

Rick deftly sidesteps any assumption that the attack was actually aimed at him. He has called the manager's bluff

and forced him to either come out from behind his façade and speak about the real issue, or let Rick get back to work while he tries to figure out what just happened.

If the manager chooses to discuss his actual concerns, even from a different attack mode, then blending, neutralizing, and guiding will become possible for Rick.

Reflecting on the Blend Step . . .

Use Tenkan as an anchor to remind you to turn and try to honestly see things from the other person's point of view.

Prove that you are attempting to understand your attacker by making a guess at what they are feeling and what needs they are trying to have met.

You will know you have blended and achieved a state of neutrality when your attacker agrees with, or makes adjustments to, your assessment of their feelings and needs.

Build a language of compassion by becoming familiar with the list of feelings. This will help you deal with the stress of a verbal attack by enabling you to search in the body language, vocal intonations, facial expressions, and the presuppositions of your attacker for the real intent of their attack.

Often the intent of an attacker is to get you to change behaviors because they are not able to accept you the way you are currently behaving.

This is often driven by the fact that your behavior is one that the attacker would not be able to accept in themselves if they were to behave in that manner. This is called projection and is a common catalyst for verbal attack

patterns. Knowing this makes it easier to blend and achieve neutrality with attackers.

CRITICAL: Learn to modulate your voice by recording it and listening objectively. This is often a blind spot for people who are frequently attacked and cannot pinpoint a reason for the attacks.

Neutralize & Guide

The next step in the *Stay CALM Method*™ is difficult to define. It is fleeting; there are no emotions connected to the step and the quest to guide can prevent us from identifying this critical point in the method. There is nothing to say or do in the neutral step; it is merely a way station on the journey towards resolution.

In the following chapter, we will attempt to point it out to you and give you a description of the conditions just before and just after neutrality, so that you might recognize it more easily. As you practice the method, you will at first notice where the neutral places were *after* the exchange has passed. In time you will be able to spot them just as they occur and have the confidence to move to the guide step with no resistance.

The Neutral Step
Neutrality is achieved when the attacker has given up the fight. This can be confirmed by the attacker agreeing with, or making a correction to, your effort to describe their feelings and needs to them. This step MUST be achieved before moving to the Guide Step. I've said that at least three times, right?

It's often easier to tell when you have *not* achieved neutrality. Some landmarks that show you still need to blend are:
1) You feel that *you* are still close to fighting or fleeing—either because you are clamming up, getting defensive, or being offensive—time to go to No-Mind.

2) You notice that the person across from you still has a lot of tension around their eyes and forehead: Make an attempt to discover what they are feeling.
3) You observe that the person across from you has stopped making contributions to the dialogue: Try Tenkan yet again.

Keep this in mind: Neutral does not mean CALM! It just means neutral. You can put a car going headlong into a wall at 90 miles an hour into neutral—and you still have to get it to stop!

Neutrality is a very brief moment along the way to CALM. Think of it as a train that is slowing down long enough just to change tracks. It is only the beginning of achieving CALM.

At this point the real work begins with your ability to guide and dialogue with your new partner.

The Guide Step

Most of us are actually very good at guiding, but because we have spent so many years trying to guide from a place of resistance rather than from a place of neutrality, we may have mistakenly decided we are not all that effective at guiding.

Additionally, our best guiding is done when we know where the other person stands. Once we have seen her point of view and know what she is actually requesting of us, guiding becomes a much simpler matter.

The most critical skill to develop, if you have not yet

Neutralize & Guide

done so, is the ability to make requests for what you need to be fulfilled in life. Making requests that are honest, and not just making polite-sounding demands, will be a primary focus for this section.

We've already seen a few samples of the request pattern in action. The key elements are expressing what we are feeling and what we need as a result of those feelings, all of which should be based on observation free from evaluation.

Let's look at all the steps in this detailed example:

Eric (Star Salesperson): Betty (Credit Dept), why have you refused credit to this new prospective client? You never help me out when I need it the most! (Remember, *never, ever, always,* and *even* are major cues that you are being attacked)

Betty: Eric, are you feeling irritated because you need to make your numbers and the credit worthiness of your prospect is standing in the way?

Eric: It's more like you're standing in the way. This company received credit from us on a previous order. I don't understand why you're denying them.

Betty: It sounds as if you are very frustrated that this may not turn into a sale for you. Are you feeling a lot of pressure?

Eric: I am. Bob's on my case and I've got to get my numbers up. You're the one person who stands between me and this sale.

Neutralize & Guide

Neutrality has been achieved even though there is some residual hostility. Eric has exposed his pain.

Here is the Guide Step:

Betty: I want to help but I would need to be able to talk with you candidly about this customer with open dialogue. Could I request that you give me a chance to explain my decision? Maybe together we can figure out how to make both our jobs a little easier and still take care of the customer.

Eric: I guess so. It just seems like lately you've been turning down all my prospects.

Betty: I wish I could approve more of your prospects. After all, when you sell more, our whole company earns more profit, which makes it better here for all of us. May I explain the reason for these turndowns?

Eric: Yeah, I guess it will help to understand why they aren't credit worthy.

Since many salespeople are Controlling Pyramids, or Squiggly Promoters, an accounting type like Betty, who is likely to be an Analyst Square, needs to exercise a high level of patience in achieving a neutral position in dealing with behaviors like Eric's.

Once Eric hears that Betty really does understand his frustration and the pressure he is facing, he is more open to hearing about the job Betty must perform in order to avoid risk for her company.

Neutralize & Guide

This attack was handled well and will result in improved relations between Betty and Eric.

Here is another example, step by step.

Girlfriend: Why are you feeding my kids McDonald's again? Don't you even care about their health?

Boyfriend: It sounds like you're really concerned, and might be thinking that I don't care about your kids. Do you need me to pick different types of food for them?

Girlfriend: Yes, please. I'd appreciate it if you'd feed them healthier foods like Subway or Togo's.

Now that the attack has been reframed as a neutral request, the right to guide has been earned. Here goes:

Boyfriend: I'm feeling a little pressure because the kids are always hounding me to take them to McDonald's. Could I ask that we talk to them together and explain that we can't always eat there?

This attack was handled well by the boyfriend, especially considering the complexity of taking care of his girlfriend's children.

As you are noticing by now the Guide Step really is fairly straightforward. What makes this step difficult is our natural instinct to resist and our automatic desire to attack back. When we can look past the attack and hear the feelings and needs that drove the person to attack in the first place, it becomes much easier to let go of our need to "be

right" and address the real issue behind the attack.

I urge you to keep a journal handy and write down any confrontations that you become involved in over the next few weeks. Reflect on the attack(s) and see if you can rewrite the scenarios, based on the three steps: Blend, Neutralize, and Guide, the core of the *Stay CALM Method*™.

At this point, I would like to make this request: Try the *Stay CALM Method*™ with the people in your life. Let them know you are attempting to communicate with better results and that you want to relate with other people more effectively. Ask for feedback from them about how you present yourself, not just what you communicate, but *how* you communicate. Can they tell that you are making an effort to really understand them without becoming defensive? When you have a breakdown and find yourself engaging in counterproductive behaviors in response to a verbal attack pattern, use that breakdown as an opportunity to achieve a lasting breakthrough in handling attacks of this sort.

Sometimes it's tough to see the value of a pile of manure when you're standing in it up over your eyes. Once it spreads and fertilizes new growth, the value becomes clear.

At the very heart of this method is your own willingness to ask better questions, both of yourself and of the people in your life. I sincerely hope the rich information in this book will help to provide some direction and a few tools to use in achieving greater harmony in your relationships (and in your relationship with yourself).

Reflection on the Stay CALM Method™

Stay CALM allows us to install a new option called "Harmonize" that will make it possible for us to see past verbal attacks and hear the real issue behind the attack. It is our <u>sincere</u> effort to understand our would-be opponent that enables us to blend with them, seeing things from their perspective, and achieve a neutral state wherein the fight ends and cooperation begins.

The Blend Step is accomplished most effectively by observing other people's behaviors without evaluating them. Separating the behaviors we observe from our judgment about those behaviors makes it much easier to stay calm, and connect with the other person in a way that avoids blame and anger.

Once we have accomplished a state of neutrality, evidenced by our attacker acknowledging or adjusting our assessment of their feelings and needs, we have earned the right to guide them to understand our own feelings and needs. The goal is to partner with our attacker and look together at other possible solutions to the issue.

The Guide Step is fairly natural for most of us and is accomplished most effectively by becoming expert at making requests without being demanding. This skill takes very little time to develop and enables us to build trusting relationships based on honesty and compassion.

Neutralize & Guide

Quick Reference to Stay CALM

Upon hearing an attack (the words *never, ever, always,* and *even* are usually in the pattern), think *TENKAN!*

This is an anchor that will remind you to:

Blend—Make an effort to determine what the other person is feeling and what needs are not being met.

Remember: Use the Four Cornerstones and the Personality Quadrant to quickly determine what the attacker is really trying to do: change your behaviors, achieve their own goals, not be wrong, or get you to like them.

Neutralize—Attacker makes a shift and acknowledges or makes adjustments to your assessment of their feelings and needs.

Remember: Do not try to guide until you have achieved a state of neutrality, since it will only meet with more resistance. If the attacker is still resistant, return to the Blend Step.

Guide—Make a request based on your feelings and needs in the situation. Do it without demanding and be open to seeking different options to create a solution in partnership with your ex-opponent.

Remember: Your ability to be compassionate and honest will create lasting trust in the relationship.

For ongoing support in using the *Stay CALM Method*™ visit www.verbalaikido.com

Debugging

Debugging

There are a couple of interpersonal glitches that I feel should be discussed in wrapping up this book.

The first is that many times in seminars, when I teach the *Stay CALM Method*™, participants are shocked at the upfront nature of this method. Our culture in America is one that abhors being direct. We are overly concerned with being politically correct and often avoid dealing with the reality of our problems because we are so obsessed with "being nice."

This condition leads to people becoming resigned to the status quo, no matter how miserable and, as a result, being bitter about their relationships, their lives, and their very existence. The result is that a lot of people complain about the condition their lives are in, but are unwilling to engage in new behaviors to change those conditions.

So here is one of the bugs in this system:

Complaints

Complaints are not attacks per se, but they have an erosive effect on the quality of our environment. Anyone who has sat through daily breaks and lunch hours or lived with a complainer for a number of years can relate to the feelings of defeat and despondency that are brought on by constant exposure to complaining.

So let's handle this bug in the system.

Debugging

Complaining occurs as an outward expression of an inner commitment or need that is not being met. When we are dealing with a complainer, we must learn to look for the commitment behind the complaint, for the unmet needs that aren't being fulfilled.

In the chapter on the Blend Step there were two examples of poorly expressed feelings that were statements of complaint. Let's look at those again and see if we can discover the commitment behind the complaint.

Sister: I feel it is useless to talk to my boyfriend. He simply refuses to listen.

The commitment that is driving the complaint is that the sister wants to have an open relationship with her boyfriend. The unexpressed feelings are despondency and maybe even desperation, and certainly frustration and a little anger. She would be fulfilled if there were clear and effective communication between them.

Employee: I feel my boss is being manipulative. He plays all of us against each other.

The commitment behind this complaint is to having a high level of trust and confidence in the relationship with his boss. The employee is trying to express feelings of inferiority, over being used and confused, and generally dissatisfied with the management style of his boss. The employee would be fulfilled if his boss made clear requests and encouraged his people to do the same.

Debugging

This is a big step in helping other people around us avoid conflict in their lives. By partnering with complainers and speaking to their commitments and not to their complaints, we can often help people connect with their true feelings and needs and give them tools to help achieve a higher degree of fulfillment in their lives.

As managers or leaders, we can create an environment of trust and confidence when we can effectively address the commitment behind our people's complaints. This one tool alone can bring a greater level of harmony into our day-to-day lives.

I recommend making a copy of the list of feelings on pages 107 and 109 to keep with you and refer to often. Become familiar with the language of feelings. Most of us are so disconnected from our feelings that when you can provide gentle coaching to help people reconnect with their own emotional state, you will quickly be identified as a peacemaker and sought out as a diplomat.

Thinking Patterns

The final bug is your own thinking patterns. The way you evaluate others, and more importantly, *the way you expect others to act is one of the primary reasons for the way people behave in your presence.*

Have you ever had someone look at you blankly when you describe the characteristics and behaviors of a mutual acquaintance? They look into their own experience and come back with "Hmmm, no . . . they aren't like that when I'm with them . . ."

Debugging

In Covey's book *The 7 Habits of Highly Effective People*, he writes about a glitch in classroom scheduling that had a class of behaviorally-challenged high school students accidentally labeled as gifted students. They were mistakenly directed to take class with a few unsuspecting teachers who assumed they were gifted students.

The school administration decided not to tell anyone and see what happened. The "challenged" students all ended up outperforming the rest of the student body by the end of the semester. When the teachers were asked what methods they employed to achieve such results, they said: "We tried our usual methodology but weren't getting the results we wanted. So we tried different techniques, knowing that these students might need to be challenged at a higher level, and they responded wonderfully."

Most people will live up or down to our expectations of them. Unless you are particularly strong willed, your concern of what others are thinking of you will drive your behavior. You'll underperform or overachieve according to the evaluation of your abilities by the authority figures or leaders in most group situations.

So when we are talking about the dynamics of changing human behavior, keep at the top of your mind that your own beliefs about another person's ability to change is, in no small part, contributing to that person's success or failure in achieving results. Even if someone is having tremendous success in some other area of his or her life, your inability or unwillingness to see the changes will

often bring about the very behaviors he or she has so proudly shifted away from when not in your presence.

This concept is so important that I'm going to put the saying on a single page:

Give people permission to show up differently.

Onward

Some things are so. We are either growing or decaying. Nothing is static. This is so. So grow.

It's as easy as that. You choose. You do it right now, in a millisecond. You make the choice to show up differently, then you *practice* that choice for the rest of your days, or until you make a new choice.

I promised a Suggested Reading list. This will put you at risk of having more "Shelf Help" books that look great in your bookcase. Remember, the only way anyone can tell you read them will be based on your results.

If any of the books you read are going to create new results in your life, you must take action. Remember that the definition of insanity is doing the same thing over and over and expecting different results. Or said another way, if you always do what you've always done, you'll always get what you've always got.

Alright already, enough soap box. Following is a list of some of the books on my shelf. They've helped not because I read them and then shelved them, but because now I focus my time and energy on helping other people to implement the lessons contained within them.

This brings me to my last bit of advice. If you want to see incredible results in your life, share these ideas and skills with other people and help them improve their lives. It's very fulfilling. A very popular author named Richard Bach said we teach best what we need to learn the most.

Thank you for helping me to learn. Writing this book has been a real gift for me. I hope it brings you amazing results too.

Suggested Reading

I am providing a simple list of books and seminars that I would suggest if you are interested in learning more about conflict resolution, communication and relationships. In this day and age of Amazon and Google I figure if you have the book title and the author's name, you can take it from there.

Self-Discovery Titles
The Attractor Factor by Joe Vitale
The Birth and Death of Meaning by Ernest Becker
Emotional Intelligence by Daniel Goleman
How to Win Friends and Influence People by Dale Carnegie
Illusions: The Adventures of a Reluctant Messiah by
    Richard Bach
The Power of Now by Eckhart Tolle

East/West and Aikido Titles
Autobiography of a Yogi by Paramhansa Yogananda

The Book of Five Rings by Miyamoto Musashi
Mentoring, Tao of Giving and Receiving by Al Chungliang Huang & Jerry Lynch
The Shambhala Guide to Aikido by John Stevens
This is It and Other Essays on Zen and Spiritual Experience by Alan Watts (any of his fine works will do, but start here)
The Way of Aikido by George Leonard
The Zen Way to the Martial Arts by Taisen Deshimaru

Communication Titles
The 48 Laws of Power by Robert Greene
Crucial Conversations by Kerry Patterson, et al
Frogs into Princes, Neuro Linguistic Programming™ by John Grinder & Richard Bandler
The Gentle Art of Verbal Self-Defense by Suzette Haden Elgin, Ph.D. (Everything in the series under this banner)
Getting to Yes by Roger Fisher & William Ury
Nonviolent Communication: A Language of Life by Marshall B. Rosenberg, Ph.D. Available from your local bookstore, or visit www.CNVC.org and www.NonviolentCommunication.com
Verbal Judo by George J. Thompson, Ph.D.
Working with Emotional Intelligence by Daniel Goleman
You Can't Teach a Kid to Ride a Bike at a Seminar by David Sandler

Leadership Titles
The Four Obsessions of an Extraordinary Executive by Patrick Lencioni

Suggested Reading

Leadership and Self-deception: Getting out of the Box by The Arbinger Institute
Primal Leadership by Daniel Goleman, et al
The Pursuit of WOW! by Tom Peters
The 7 Habits of Highly Successful People by Stephen Covey
Synchronicity, the Inner Path of Leadership by Joseph Jaworski

Really Important Seminars

Any of the public seminars and/or distance learning programs from the Arbinger Institute (www.arbinger.com)
Dale Carnegie Training (www.dalecarnegie.com)
Joe Vitale—Executive Mentoring Program (www.hypnoticmarketinginc.com)
Landmark Education—The Landmark Forum (www.landmarkeducation.com)
Psi Seminars—Entire Curriculum (www.psiseminars.com)
Sandler Sales Training (www.sandler.com)

About iCAN International

Jon Forrest is the CEO of iCAN International, LLC, a family of companies focused on creating Harmony at Work™ through better interpersonal communications and smarter strategy and business processes. Jon believes that the number one obstacle standing in the way of achieving higher levels of customer satisfaction is ineffective interdepartmental communication and inconsistent communication and execution of business strategy across the workforce. iCAN International is founded on the powerful principles described in the *Stay CALM Method*™.

iCAN International provides mind-opening and memorable tools through training, along with powerful coaching and sensible consulting in a proprietary, blended process. This approach encourages people to take a proactive stance and begin to eliminate negative group-think (Us vs. Them), and instead, work towards creating an environment of "We", where "what is right" takes precedence over "who is wrong." When everyone working for an organization aligns their focus on improving customer experience and generating more new, satisfied customers at a profit, businesses thrive and grow.

The Power of iCAN

The simple question: "What can I do to make things better

here?" takes the individual out of the blame game, the finger pointing and justification of their ineffective performance and poor results on the job. In one simple question: "How can I adjust to the changes and make things better here?", that same employee is able to take a proactive stance and make responsible choices which in turn create sustained growth and increased employee and customer satisfaction. When people have the tools, the self confidence and the support to say "I CAN make a difference." the earnings/cost savings per employee will nearly always improve.

To connect with or learn more about how iCAN International can help people in your work environment Stay CALM and produce better results, call 800.508.iCAN or visit www.icaninternational.com.

iCAN Media Publishing

Committed to the creation and distribution of multi-media products for opening minds, iCAN Media is the product and marketing company in the iCAN International family of companies. iCAN Media takes the *Stay CALM Method*™ and other works into the mainstream via unique "message vehicles" containing powerful lessons delivered in unique ways to make those lessons easy to remember and apply, even under stress.

To learn more about the iCAN Media products or to place orders for *Stay CALM* the book, please call 800.508.iCAN or visit www.icanmedia.tv.

The Products of iCAN Media

The concept of our product mix is to provide a complete system developing new behaviors through skills development. We know from experience that it takes a series of repetitions of the *Stay CALM Method*™ in various modes, visual, auditory and kinesthetic to create new habits. In order to connect through all three of the human information channels, we offer the *Stay CALM Method*™ as the book you are reading now, as a CD Rom, e-book and the best daily reminder of all, a flash card version called Mem-Cards-Books in a Flash.

Mem-Cards is a deck of 28 cards which puts each important concept and point from the book on one playing card. On the back of the card are relevant quotes and an animated version of the Tenkan Flip-Art™. The deck comes with a clear vinyl carrying wallet with a sleeve to place the "lesson for the day" card in so you can review it constantly throughout the day.

The audio version has been recorded to CD ROM and is read by the author. Play it in your car so you can listen while you drive, or download it to any MP3 player. The e-book version puts the flip art right on your desktop as an animated file and the content can be downloaded to any popular digital e-book reader.

Together, all these products comprise a complete behavior enhancement program which, after a 30 to 60 day immersion, will permanently enhance the ease and grace with which you manage conversations without them turning into confrontations, and create agreements instead of arguments.

Please look over the product offer form on the following page. You might want to buy a deck of the Mem-cards for the co-worker or family member that needs a little "CALM" support. These are perfect as a low-pressure way of letting folks around you (your manager? your executive team? your mother?) know that you are looking at tools to enhance communication in every area of your life.

To order products or learn more about how iCAN Media could help people in your work world open their minds call 800.508.iCAN or visit www.icanmedia.tv.

Quick Order Form

Use this form to order additional Stay CALM™ books and products directly from iCAN Media at a special reduced rate. Use any of the methods listed below.

Fax Orders: send this completed form to 949.453.0903.
Telephone orders: call 800.508.iCAN, toll free. Have your credit card ready.
Online orders: visit www.icanmedia.tv
Postal orders: send this completed form to:
iCAN Media, 16485 Laguna Canyon Rd., Suite 110, Irvine CA 92618

Use this order form and receive a 25% discount off the list price found in stores. If purchasing via online or telephone, be sure to mention discount code **SCOF1**.

ORDER FORM

Stay CALM™	Qty		Price	Amount
Paperback book	____	@	$12.95	____
Audio/CD version	____	@	19.95	____
e-book (for e-book readers)	____	@	11.95	____
Mem-cards (Stay CALM flash cards)	____	@	9.95	____
Stay CALM™ kit (book, CD, Mem-cards, e-book)	____	@	39.95	____

A $54 VALUE!

Sales tax: Please add 7.75% for products shipped to California addresses ____
For orders from outside the U.S., please call 949.453.0902   **Total $** ____

Name: _____

Address: _____

City: _____ State: ____ Zip: _____

Telephone: _____

Email: _____

Payment: ☐Check or ☐Visa ☐MasterCard ☐AMEX

Name on Card: _____

Card Number: _____ Exp. date: ____

Signature: _____

Total your order carefully.

Please write legibly.

Fill in all required info.

Please allow 2 weeks for shipping.

SCOF1

www.ingramcontent.com/pod-product-compliance
Lightning Source LLC
LaVergne TN
LVHW021711060526
838200LV00050B/2608